KNOWLEDGE
LEADERSHIP

KNOWLEDGE LEADERSHIP
Tools for Executive Leaders

C. Lakshman

Response
Business books from SAGE
Los Angeles ■ London ■ New Delhi ■ Singapore
www.sagepublications.com

First published in 2008 by

 Response Books
Business books from SAGE
B1/I-1 Mohan Cooperative Industrial Area
Mathura Road, New Delhi 110 044, India

SAGE Publications Inc
2455 Teller Road
Thousand Oaks, California 91320, USA

SAGE Publications Ltd
1 Oliver's Yard, 55 City Road
London EC1Y 1SP, United Kingdom

SAGE Publications Asia-Pacific Pte Ltd
33 Pekin Street
#02-01 Far East Square
Singapore 048763

Published by Vivek Mehra for SAGE Publications, typeset in 11/14pt Minion by Star Compugraphics Private Limited, Delhi and printed at Chaman Enterprises, New Delhi.

Library of Congress Cataloging-in-Publication Data

Lakshman, C.
    Knowledge leadership: tools for executive leaders/C. Lakshman.
       p. cm.
    Includes bibliographical references.
    1. Knowledge management.   2. Leadership—Case studies   I. Title.

HD30.2.L34   658.4'092—dc22   2008   2008039936

ISBN: 978-81-7829-887-0 (PB)

The SAGE Team: Sugata Ghosh, Sushmita Banerjee and Trinankur Banerjee

To
The Spirit of Innovative Knowledge Leaders

CONTENTS

LIST OF TABLES

LIST OF FIGURES

PREFACE

For a number of years now there is an increasing sense of realization among corporations and their executives that knowledge creation and dissemination is a foremost priority for the purpose of achieving a competitive advantage. Having a serious interest in top executive leadership, I began to sense that in such an environment characterized by the importance of knowledge to competitive advantage, very little attention is given to this issue within the area of leadership knowledge. I set out to investigate the role of top executives in knowledge management within their organizations and was pleasantly surprised to see quite a bit of knowledge leadership being exhibited by the executives of the corporations in the world, regardless of where they were located. I made up my mind in those early days that I would soon bring this knowledge leadership to light in the form of a book that would serve to inspire the next generation of knowledge leaders. I firmly believe that the innovative knowledge leaders of tomorrow can provide solutions to the challenges posed by the instensification of the knowledge economy around the world. Thus, this book has been in the making for at least ten years now, both in thought and in action.

I began the intellectual quest to understand the concept of leadership when I first read Lee Iacocca's autobiography, during my undergraduate days at the Engineering College and while preparing for a career in Industrial Marketing. Leaders of various sorts have interested me over my entire life. When I started working on my doctoral dissertation at Southern Illinois University, Carbondale, I had all these thoughts running through my mind about the importance of knowledge management in organizations and the crucial role of executives in undertaking such initiatives. My PhD alma mater has a strong intellectual tradition of leadership with a series of leadership conferences and seminars, with a number of publications, all establishing and strengthening the tradition. I decided to step up to the challenge of not bringing the tradition to disrepute and endeavored to do better than my previous efforts to accomplish this purpose. Thus, in this book I present, with firm conviction and strong belief, the concepts of micro and macro knowledge leadership. I sincerely hope that the readers would find this book useful in their personal lives and organizational capacities.

ACKNOWLEDGEMENTS

I am deeply indebted to all my teachers and guides for encouraging me all through and serving as an inspiration for my efforts. They are so many in number that I cannot list them individually. In addition to my teachers and guides, I am indebted to a number of other people for intellectual inspiration. The knowledge leaders and their actions discussed in this book are the ones to whom I take my hat off. Without these progressive leaders, it would have been very difficult for me to even start my research work.

I sincerely acknowledge the contributions of Professor Ronaldo Parente with whom I co-authored a study on supplier-focused knowledge management in the Brazilian auto industry. Our chance meeting at a seminar sowed the seed for our ongoing partnership, he made an immense contribution in shaping chapter 6 of this book. The book would have been incomplete had I not met him.

I sincerely acknowledge the patience and supportive encouragement of my dearest wife Sangeetha and our son Nikhil. Without their patience and understanding of my long hours away from home, this work would never have seen the light of day. I also express my thankfulness towards my other family members and friends.

1

INTRODUCTION

Expanding our information base is critical to our achieving goals: Medco has data on 38 million patients, which allow us to learn a lot more about how our drugs are prescribed and used and, ultimately, how effective they are in fighting disease. Whether it is cutting edge scientific information or the reams of data on how doctors prescribe Merck products, information lies at the heart of what the company does. Our ability to leverage information will set us apart.

—P. Roy Vagelos, Merck
(In an interview with Nancy Nichols, *HBR*, 1994)

The 21st century has brought much of the world firmly into the throes of the knowledge economy. Advances in computing technology, the internet, e-commerce and more recently m-commerce are firmly taking root in much of the world today. Humanity's collective knowledge of executive and managerial leadership has not kept pace with this change in the business context. Leadership skills development programs still predominantly focus on behavioral, interpersonal, and communication issues. Although these are still relevant, they are hardly sufficient in today's e-economy contexts. Markets around the world today are characterized by increasing levels of consumerism, which has led to high-levels of differentiation. Managers who were once managing eight brands are now faced with a situation of having to manage 80 brands in the same product category. Organizations limited to domestic market presence are now forced to operate internationally for having decent levels of competitive stability. Any and all managerial work in such environments is faced with increased information load and task complexity. Managing in this complex environment with high information loads requires special tools. Integrating information and knowledge across the organization can provide such tools to boost managerial careers and organizational competitive advantage.

This first chapter lays the foundational framework of the economic context of today's global business, thereby underlining the critical importance of the required change in leadership practices. The world has moved from an agrarian economy to an industrial economy and, further through, to a knowledge and information economy. Although the rapidity of the transition from one type of economy to the other varies from country to country, not necessarily divided by the level of development, almost all economies have experienced both of these shifts to varying degrees. Some countries such as India have the unique position of simultaneously seeing all three types of economies in operation, thereby increasing the complexity for top executives and others in the profession of management. The huge upheaval and shift in managerial practices in the transition from an agrarian to an industrial economy and the associated travails are all too well-known to be repeated in this context. The history of the field of management bears evidence of both the triumphs and travails associated with this economic transition. Likewise, the transition from the industrial economy to the information economy has left many organizations dead and obsolete, akin to the death and destruction caused by a tsunami in its wake. The fundamental rules of business and leadership of such business have changed. Knowledge is a prized asset, some of which needs to be protected at any cost, while some has to be shared for it to flourish and thrive or be forever lost. There is a competitive advantage in knowledge and information, both for the organizations and for the executives that populate them.

Despite their importance to organizations, the long tradition of leadership theory and research, and the collective base of knowledge on leadership have not addressed the role of leaders in managing information and knowledge. Consequently, information and knowledge management as key leader functions have not been explored until recently. The growing literature on information and knowledge management has repeatedly stressed the lack of leadership support for the failure of many knowledge management projects. Moreover, this literature stresses the importance of leadership for the success of information and knowledge management projects. Thus, the potential for integrating the leadership literature with information and knowledge management literature is great and is likely to be beneficial for both theory and practice. In this book, the author exploits these knowledge bases in an attempt to generate practical knowledge of the role of leaders in knowledge management through an analysis of the collective experience of successful executives of global corporations.

Although the collective wisdom on the functions of top managers has identified and emphasized the importance of the informational role of top managers, and the importance of information to create a vision, these attempts have not focused on the management of information or knowledge as key leadership roles. In addition, although some taxonomic approaches to leader behavior description have stressed and incorporated the information search and acquisition, and use of information in problem solving behaviors of leaders, this work remains at a nascent stage and needs further development. Collective wisdom also identifies the design and building of information systems as a key leader activity leading to improved organizational performance. Despite such early attempts, systematic knowledge gathering on the role of leaders in information and knowledge management is lacking. This book makes an attempt to take a first step in this direction by building a knowledge base of the role of leaders in information and knowledge management, grounded in the collective experience of some successful top executives, and establishes it as a critical leadership role that can have a significant impact on their organizations.

Neither the leadership literature nor the Knowledge Management literature has focused on the organization-wide and ongoing management of information and knowledge in terms of its positive impact on organizations. The Knowledge Management literature focuses on specific projects built using specific Knowledge Management Architectures and discrete applications as opposed to organization-wide and ongoing application. From a leadership point of view, it would be essential to manage information and knowledge on an organization-wide basis and on a continuous basis for it to be of benefit to the organization.

This book draws on the author's findings from the research done by him in the last decade, and it identifies and neatly encapsulates various practical aspects of Knowledge Leadership that provide key tools for executives of budding organizations. In one of the studies of the research program, the author performs a comparative analysis of 37 in-depth interviews of CEOs who have managed information and knowledge to drive their companies to a position of competitive advantage (Lakshman 2007a). All the 37 interviews used in this comparative study are sourced from the *Harvard Business Review*. These executive interviews were published over a long period of time in the journal and were conducted by different interviewers at different points in time. These *acquired interviews* and their use in the analysis of leaders is quite common in the realm of political leadership. The analysis in this book follows a set of criteria that can be used in the systematic study of leadership issues and help in performing such research in a systematic and scientific fashion. The criteria used in the study include representativeness of the verbal output of the sample, clear definition of the categories or constructs to be assessed from the interview content, assessment of theory-based constructs, comparability with other actors (executives in this case), and standardized content samples to ensure comparability of sources of content. The key topics of interest in this study are Leadership and Knowledge Management, the nexus of which provides the seed for the pragmatic concept of Knowledge Leadership. This study provides a blend of theory-based and experience-based knowledge to determine and establish the use of Knowledge Management tools and activities by executive leaders of organizations. Collective wisdom on leadership suggests that the *informational role* is one of the many legitimate roles played by executive leaders. One of the key findings in this study is that a leader's realization of the significance of knowledge and information sharing is a critical precursor to the roles played by the leader in managing information and knowledge.

A number of case studies and research approaches have been utilized by the author in piecing together this knowledge compendium. Knowledge Leadership not only by top executives but also by lower level managers is a significant topic of concern addressed by the author in Chapter 4. Knowledge Leadership in multiple parts of the *value-chain* is addressed in Chapters 5 and 6. Knowledge Leadership is demonstrated through multiple-case studies of executives working in different industrial sectors. In all, a comprehensive treatment of the concept of Knowledge Leadership and its associated tools are provided in this book.

Based on in-depth investigations of highly successful executive leaders from Jack Welch to Michael Dell, and examinations of global industries from automobile to retail based in continents from Asia to South and North America, this book consolidates the best Knowledge Leadership practices to create a reservoir of knowledge for executives. The content is organized into 12 chapters, each focusing on a different dimension of Knowledge Leadership, suited for a broad range of executive backgrounds. Chapter 2 describes the new leadership imperatives of the knowledge economy, while also providing a practical blend of wisdom on knowledge management and executive leadership. Chapter 3 provides a basic structure of Knowledge Leadership and its key dimensions. Using such a structure, this chapter outlines the primary mechanisms that top executives can use along each of the dimensions of Knowledge Leadership.

Chapter 4 focuses on interpersonal Knowledge Leadership that helps managers at all levels to utilize the newfound knowledge in information and knowledge management to improve their range of influence over subordinates and significant others in their organizations. Chapter 5 provides top executives with a key set of knowledge management strategies that can be used vis-à-vis customers. This chapter identifies the instrumental role of customer-focused knowledge management in spiraling Dell Inc. to new heights. Chapter 6 focuses on the other side of the value-chain by detailing supplier-focused knowledge management practices of companies in the Brazilian auto industry.

Chapter 7 examines one of the most hailed top executives of corporate America (viz., Jack Welch) to identify and explicate the role of executives in knowledge management and their knowledge-based strategies in organizations. This chapter reveals that effective leaders play an active role in Knowledge Leadership through mechanisms, such as destroying the Not Invented Here (NIH) syndrome, instituting programs of knowledge transfer, and establishing knowledge-based human resource strategies and IT based knowledge management systems. Chapter 8 describes rural Knowledge Leadership in practice through ITC top executive Y.C. Deveshwar's initiative of e-choupals and the revolution it is bringing about in the corporate world.

Chapter 9 turns its attention to global Knowledge Leadership and how Percy Barnevik of Asea Brown Boveri (ABB) utilized it in the form of matrix management to execute its strategy in more than 40 countries around the world. The retail industry is part of a very hot and emerging sector in many parts of the world. Chapter 10 describes supplier-focused and customer-oriented knowledge management strategies of certain key Asian entrepreneurs in the global retail scenario. Chapter 11 describes a cluster of knowledge-based performance management strategies that would provide valuable additions to any executive's tool kit in improving performance of subordinate managers. Chapter 12 gives attention to Knowledge Leadership practices in the not-for-profit world using cases of community hospitals, police departments, and environmental organizations.

2

LEADERSHIP IMPERATIVES FOR THE KNOWLEDGE ECONOMY

The technology available today really boosts the value of information sharing. We can share design databases and methodologies with supplier-partners in ways that just weren't possible five to ten years ago. This speeds time to market—often dramatically—and creates a lot of value that can be shared between buyer and supplier.

—Michael Dell, Dell Inc.
(In an interview with J. Margretta, *HBR*, 1998)

H aving outlined the broad changes in the economic context of business in the previous chapter, we now turn our attention to the current state of knowledge on leadership and identify the required changes in them. There are three major problems with current conceptualizations of leadership that motivate and lend guidance to this treatise on executive (knowledge) leadership. First, the extant conceptualizations of leadership approach the topic from the point of view of effectiveness of different styles of leadership and assume that what leaders do is captured comprehensively by the 'styles' of leadership. Given that some experts in the leadership area identify a role for leaders in information and knowledge management, but very little subsequent research exists to substantiate or further investigate this aspect of leadership, the assumption that we know what leaders (especially executive leaders) do is questionable. Styles of leadership do have connections to knowledge leadership at non-executive levels which are described in a subsequent chapter. Thus, when the present author initiated his research, a reexamination of what executive leaders do, with specific reference to their knowledge management roles was long overdue.

Second, the dominant organizational behavior approach to leadership theory has focused on the individual, dyadic, and small group level of analysis. Thus, with the probable exception of charismatic theories, leadership at the top managerial level in organizations has not been systematically examined. It is not clear whether the theoretical frameworks used at the micro-levels are applicable at the macro-levels in the organization. Seeing leadership as primarily an interpersonal phenomenon leaves much to be desired in terms of the practical lessons we can draw for leadership of entire organizations and not just a group of individuals. Hence, there is a significant need for a book on strategic leadership in the specific context of Knowledge Management.

Third, the traditional theories of leadership do not focus on leadership processes as much as they do on leadership styles and their effectiveness. The extant theories of leadership are lacking significantly because of the dominant focus on cross-sectional analysis and focus on content to the exclusion of processes, which are inherently longitudinal. The approach of generalizing from the practices of successful executives, used here, serves to identify the leadership processes over time and their actions that have an impact on the organizations which can be of higher practical significance. This book aims to overcome these drawbacks of the extant approaches to leadership and thus provides answers to the following questions. What do leaders at higher levels in organizations (such as Chief Executive Officers [CEOs]) do? What role, if any, do such leaders play in managing information and knowledge in the organizations? What are the processes through which leaders effect information and knowledge management? And finally, what impact does it have on organizational effectiveness and leadership perceptions?

LEADERSHIP: CURRENT STATE OF KNOWLEDGE

The current state of collective wisdom on leadership can be broadly divided into four categories. The four broad approaches to the examination of leaders and leadership, namely, the trait approach, the behavior approach, the contingency approach, and the transformational and charismatic approach have given very little emphasis to the information and knowledge management aspects of leadership. Some of the specific components of the approaches do imply a role of leaders in knowledge management but fall short of examining Knowledge Management systematically. First, the trait approach does identify business knowledge (a component of Knowledge Management) as an essential quality of effective leaders. Second, the behavioral and contingency approaches to leadership suggest that information search and acquisition, and information use are core dimensions of leader behavior that have an impact on performance. Third, information and knowledge requirements of situations are also key contingencies that impact leader behavior.

The behavior of the leaders in facilitating the existence and availability of required information and knowledge through such processes as Knowledge Management can have a significant impact on organizational effectiveness. Finally, the charismatic approach implies that information acquisition and analysis is important for the development of vision in organizations. More importantly, knowledge management processes may be more systematic than the charismatic appeal mechanism in obtaining shared vision in organizations on an organization-wide basis. Thus, current wisdom points to the significance of the examination of the processes through which executive leaders manage knowledge in their organizations to obtain positions of competitive advantage.

KNOWLEDGE MANAGEMENT

Our purpose here is to primarily identify the importance of knowledge management to organizations and then subsequently to identify the constituent components of Knowledge Management to illustrate the use of such components in the organizations represented by the CEOs (cases) included here. Knowledge has become a key corporate resource and the necessity to manage that resource has become crucial. The difficulty of managing this resource has made it a critical leadership role. Several Knowledge Management experts have documented the importance of the management of information and knowledge to the effective performance of organizations including leading organizations to competitive advantage. Organizational experts have long since realized the value of information and knowledge through means such as modeling organizations as interpretive systems and knowledge-creating mechanisms, and through the specification of concepts like organizational memory and organizational learning.

Knowledge Management experts draw a systematic connection between stimuli, data, information, and knowledge, with knowledge occupying the highest semiotic level. According to dictionaries, knowledge is the accumulation and understanding of facts, ideas, principles, or skills. Knowledge has also been referred in terms of a set of beliefs about causal relationships between actions and their probable consequences, or alternatively as information that has been placed in its context and thus has been formatted to make sense. Other experts have argued that information becomes knowledge either through some transformation processes within organizations or a discernment process on the part of individuals. Thus, there is the explicit realization that information is converted to knowledge through a broad range of processes, such as Nonaka's knowledge creation spiral (Nonaka and Takeuchi 1995) involving the interaction between tacit and explicit knowledge, moving through multiple levels within organizations. Here, I provide a basic description of Knowledge Management to which the rest of the book will adhere to.

What is Knowledge Management?

Knowledge Management is defined as an organizational capability that allows people in organizations—working as individuals, or in teams, projects, or other such communities of interest—to create, capture, share, and leverage their collective knowledge to improve performance. It can simultaneously be conceptualized as the concern for the creation of structures that combine the most advanced elements of technological resources and the indispensable input of human response and decision-making. Putting processes in place containing a massive amount of information, organizing it logically, and making it accessible to the right people are all key components of such a view of Knowledge Management. Internal benchmarking efforts to share knowledge-creating strategic alliances, investments in training and development, and the building of computer based information repositories and systems are all key components of Knowledge Management. Some experts have identified two broad approaches (strategies) to the management of knowledge in organizations, namely, the personalization approach and the codification approach. The personalization approach would include face-to-face communication; communication through structures, such as networks of people, cross-functional teams, committees, task forces, training and development; internal knowledge sharing through benchmarking and job rotation; and creation of strategic alliances. The codification approach refers to the technological route for knowledge management and would include the setting up of databases, data warehouses, decision support systems, Enterprise Resource Planning (ERP) systems, and electronic networks for communication and sharing knowledge.

In the rest of this book, Knowledge Management is conceptualized as the overall set of processes that are put in place for the purpose of identifying sources of relevant data and information in organizations, the eventual conversion of these data and information to knowledge, and their subsequent dissemination to different points in the organization where they are needed. Knowledge Management can be operationalized through the existence of extensive networks (both social and technological) at multiple levels in or throughout the organization. Such operationalization is important from the perspective of identifying leader behaviors in the Knowledge Management realm by grounding it in the successful practices of executives.

Components of Knowledge Management

Teams

The use of a team based organizational design, with extensive use of cross-functional and cross-divisional teams can be seen as the manifestation of the extensive organization-wide networks. Bringing together different people with potentially diverse data and information through teams, enhances and facilitates the process of management of information relevant to decision-making, and the process of conversion of data and information to knowledge that can then be codified using technology. Additionally, teams also are the means through which crucial tacit knowledge can be brought to the surface. Tacit knowledge is that which cannot be codified or documented, but resides in the minds of the executives, having been acquired through years of practice and experience. Tacit knowledge can be converted to explicit knowledge only through transformation processes that include intensive interaction of people such as in work teams. Moreover, teams are essential not only from the point of view of generating knowledge, but also from the point of view of disseminating knowledge in the organization.

Other components

In addition, other processes that are set up for the specific enhancement of the data and information obtained by the key informants identified earlier from various entities in the environment such as customers and suppliers constitute a key component of Knowledge Management. Such practices as locating employees on the shop floor of customer organizations or simpler practices as key executives spending a significant amount of time with their customers can serve as vital sources of accurate information that are of use to the focal organization. Extensive use of e-mail networks, developing strategic alliances for the purpose of learning, developing forums of interaction with different groups of constituents, job rotation and personnel transfers, ongoing training and development efforts, sharing knowledge through written documents are other mechanisms of Knowledge Management in organizations. Many strategic alliances and joint ventures for knowledge acquisition purposes use many of the aforementioned mechanisms for successful knowledge transfer and subsequent dissemination.

Executives across the length and breadth of the organizations intending to be successful have to first acquire and possess business or process knowledge in their own domains or across multiple domains. Aspiring executives, desiring to exhibit knowledge leadership, will also have to identify the people in various parts of their organization, who have access to key pieces of information and knowledge, on an ongoing basis, by virtue of their position and the people they interact with. Once this identification is done, the aspiring executive will have to form communities of learning with these key individuals as members. Executives desiring to practice knowledge leadership will have to build their repertoire of information search and acquisition behaviors by utilizing such key informants, among other similar attempts for acquiring knowledge. These executives will also need to practice their "information use in problem solving" behaviors to make practical use of such information. Successful knowledge leaders will also extend these practices beyond themselves by institutionalizing such practices throughout the units they are responsible for. Possessing managerial motivations, such as need for power, need for achievement, and personality characteristics, such as charisma, high-levels of self-confidence, drive, enthusiasm, and integrity, may not be sufficient in the complex realities of the 21st century. These traits and motivations have to be exploited by exercising the multiple mechanisms to create, share, and leverage knowledge for competitiveness. Instituting practices of internal and external benchmarking of processes, explicit knowledge sharing initiatives, investing in training and (managerial) development practices, establishing well thought out practices of job rotation and personnel transfer for knowledge sharing purposes, in addition to leveraging technological resources such as e-mail networks, and knowledge management systems are all part of the broad set of imperatives for effective leadership in this modern world.

3

KNOWLEDGE LEADERSHIP

WHAT CAN TOP EXECUTIVES DO?

It is the key to being able to identify opportunities that others might not see and to exploit those opportunities rapidly and fully. This means that in order to generate extraordinary value for shareholders, a company has to learn better than its competitors and apply that knowledge throughout its businesses faster and more widely than they do. The way we see it, anyone in the organization who is not directly accountable for making a profit should be involved in creating and distributing knowledge that the company can use to make a profit.

The top management team must stimulate the organization, not control it. Its role is to provide strategic directives, to encourage learning, and to make sure there are mechanisms for transferring the lessons. The role of leaders at all levels is to demonstrate to people that they are capable of achieving more than they can achieve and that they should never be satisfied with where they are now.

—John Browne, British Petroleum
(In an interview with S.E. Prokesch, *HBR*, 1997)

THE ROLE OF LEADERSHIP
IN KNOWLEDGE MANAGEMENT

M any Knowledge Management experts have identified leadership as a key variable in the relationship between knowledge management and organizational effectiveness. Much of the evidence for the positive impact of knowledge management on organizations is in the form of operational improvements limited to specific processes and functions. Experts argue for broader knowledge management initiatives that are enterprise wide as opposed to specific applications. More importantly, knowledge management should be seen as an ongoing process of doing business and thus should not be limited to discrete steps using specific applications, but institutionalized as a continuous process to serve the organization's needs. This challenging aspect of making knowledge management continuous and ongoing is therefore a key leadership responsibility. Cleveland addressed this issue of the role of leadership in managing knowledge in his book, *The Knowledge Executive* (1985). He stresses the need for the use of teams, communities of people, and other such networks as the role for leaders in managing information and knowledge, in conformance with the components of knowledge management identified earlier. Other experts have addressed the organizational issues and the need to have strategies to manage knowledge. Since it is generally accepted that the CEOs have the main responsibility for strategic management, the role of leadership in knowledge management follows from the strategic responsibilities of the CEO.

One of the questions I promised to answer earlier in the book with respect to what leaders do is discussed here. Specifically, the role of leaders in information and knowledge management is identified and described through an analysis of multiple cases of successful top executive knowledge leadership. This role of leaders in information and knowledge management is accomplished through the two broad routes, namely, technology and social networks. The current wisdom on leadership is supplemented by such systematic analysis of executive knowledge leadership cases. Through a combination of the review of current leadership and knowledge management wisdom and an analysis of CEO interviews, I identify and expound on some practical lessons of Knowledge Leadership. The rest of the chapter describes five important lessons about Knowledge Leadership collated from some of the studies conducted by the author. These five lessons are as follows:

1. Executives should first and foremost realize the value and significance of Knowledge Leadership and what and how it can contribute to higher organizational performance. Studies have repeatedly found that the more successful executives have a strong realization of the importance of Knowledge Leadership and use it to effectively advance their businesses.

2. Having realized the value and significance of Knowledge Leadership, executives then turn their attention to using two well-known means to establish Knowledge Management practices in their organizations. They use both social and technological means to manage knowledge by instituting the appropriate processes in their organizations, constantly encouraging people to use these two mechanisms, leading by example in using these routes, and reinforcing people for their contribution to these two mechanisms. The social route to Knowledge Leadership is achieved by using teams and learning communities, knowledge transfer practices from within and outside the organization, and carefully planned job rotation and personnel transfer practices for knowledge objectives. The technological route to Knowledge Leadership is achieved by establishing information systems, knowledge transfer mechanisms, and practices of sharing these mechanisms with as many people as possible and necessary within the organization, not to mention those outside the organization (relevant groups). There is sufficient evidence to suggest that

organizations with such knowledge leaders bring about higher levels of performance all around, including the achievement of a competitive edge in the marketplace.

3. One of the more important lessons learnt from successful executives engaging in Knowledge Leadership is that they have an intense customer-focused approach and inspire others to have the same. More specifically, successful executives translate this customer-focused approach to vastly improve information and knowledge transfer through the channels between the organization and their customers. Again, these executives encourage others in the organization to engage in two-way sharing of information and knowledge between the organization and their customers, lead by personal example in this regard, and reinforce such behaviors of people in this domain of Knowledge Leadership. These practices are also known to relate strongly to organizational performance that is sustainable in the long run.

4. Successful executives engaging in Knowledge Leadership identify both internal and external customers that are the targets of the intense customer-focus. They establish channels of information and knowledge flow thereby creating opportunities for other managers in their organizations to utilize these channels (opportunities) to engage in higher levels of knowledge creation, transfer, leverage, and dissemination. It is a little known fact that Japan's automobile, semiconductor, consumer electronics, and other industries have achieved world class status as a result of such focus on internal and external customers and extensive knowledge movement through these aforementioned channels.

5. As in any economic context, leadership ultimately depends on the personal example set by the top executives in showing enthusiasm and active participation in the channels of information and knowledge flow established for that purpose. This personal participation and example setting is what gets the

rest of the organization going in making these knowledge-leveraging practices more effective. These five lessons are described in further detail in the rest of the chapter, including some information on the systematic approach used in distilling these practices.

Knowledge Leadership Concepts and Practices for Top Executives

This book accomplishes what many experts have strongly called for in the examination of leadership practices for the 21st century knowledge economy contexts. Such examination of leadership practices entails more qualitative and processual approaches, including detailed multiple-case analysis, in the examination of leadership processes. The Knowledge Leadership practices identified and developed here have been found to be productive in a number of cases across nations and industrial contexts. Thus Knowledge Leadership is firmly grounded in modern day reality. Constant comparative analysis of multiple cases is an essential feature of the method behind the practices espoused here.

In this chapter, the key focus is on executive leaders and their use of Knowledge Management in effectively leading their organizations to high performance. Hence the criterion of appropriate sampling suggests the use of CEOs or other leaders in organizations with broad organizational responsibilities. In-depth interviews have been a key component of most qualitative investigations and are a key component of data collection in the multiple-case analysis method used here. I specifically describe a constant comparative analysis of 37 CEOs of global corporations in the form of identifying patterns and trends across the subjects to identify emerging relationships that constitute the kernels of learning and wisdom on Knowledge Leadership. Scientific principles of grounded theory, theoretical sampling, and theoretical saturation were adhered to in this process of generating the kernels of wisdom on Knowledge Leadership.[1]

The findings of one of the studies in the author's research program leading to an identification and development of the Knowledge Leadership practices are described here. This study comparatively analyzed 37 in-depth interviews with CEOs of corporations that have been successful in their knowledge management activities. These in-depth interviews were conducted by different authors and were published in the *Harvard Business Review* at different points in time. I subjected all interviews to the following selection criteria listed to qualify for inclusion in the study: (*a*) all interviews were to be with the CEO or some other top official with broad organizational responsibilities, and not someone with functional responsibilities such as the Chief Financial Officer (CFO) or Chief Information Officer (CIO); (*b*) all interviews with the CEO or other top official were pertaining to the CEO's tenure at a single organization and should not have been about his/her general experience with many companies; and (*c*) all interviews were to address broad organizational concerns including knowledge management and should not have focused exclusively on the CEO or exclusively on one function or few functions within the organizations. Based on these criteria, several interviews were not included. Table 3.1 provides a list of all the CEO interviews included in the study.

Comparisons were made across these 37 CEOs and their organizations. Subsequently, the organizational features of the companies represented by these CEOs were identified and generalizations were made for developing a set of successful Knowledge Leadership practices. To ensure accuracy of the information obtained from these interviews, multiple sources of such information including organizational documents were used to check for its veracity. The data from all 37 interviews is available to a large extent from varied sources and serves as a corollary to the sources used in this study. For example, the information pertaining to Dell is available from a number of sources and thus attests for its validity. Information about Ford obtained from the *Harvard Business Review* (*HBR*) interview is in agreement with another independent interview with Nasser and a *Fortune* magazine article that describes some aspects of

Table 3.1

Names and Positions of the Executives included in the Study

	Name(s) of Interviewee(s)	Position in Organization	Company Represented	Name(s) of Interviewer(s)	Date of Publication in the HBR
1.	Jack Welch	CEO	General Electric (GE)	Noel Tichy and Ram Charan	September–October 1989
2.	Yoshihisa Tabuchi	CEO	Nomura Securities	Michael Schrage	July–August 1989
3.	George Fisher	CEO	Motorola, Inc.	Bernard Avishai and William Taylor	November–December 1989
4.	Paul Cook	Chairman and CEO	Raychem	William Taylor	March–April 1990
5.	Alain Gomez	CEO	Thomson, S.A.	Janice McCormick and Nan Stone	May–June 1990
6.	Rod Canion	CEO	Compaq	Alan Webber	July–August 1990
7.	Robert Haas	Chairman and CEO	Levi Strauss & Co.	Robert Howard	September–October 1990
8.	John Reed	CEO	Citicorp	Noel Tichy and Ram Charan	November–December 1990
9.	Raymond Smith	CEO	Bell Atlantic	Rosabeth Moss Kanter	January–February 1991
10.	Percy Barnevik	CEO	ABB	William Taylor	March–April 1991
11.	Lee P. Brown	Commissioner of Police	New York City Police Department	Alan Webber	May–June 1991
12.	Carl Hahn	CEO	Volkswagen	Bernard Avishai	July–August 1991
13.	Robert F. McDermott	CEO	USAA	Thomas Teal	September–October 1991
14.	Arnold Hiatt	Chairman	Stride Rite	Nan Stone	March–April 1992
15.	Arden C. Sims	CEO	Globe Metallurgical Inc.	Bruce Rayner	May–June 1992
16.	Phil Knight	CEO	Nike	Geraldine E. Willigan	July–August 1992

(Table 3.1 continued)

(*Table 3.1 continued*)

	Name(s) of Interviewee(s)	Position in Organization	Company Represented	Name(s) of Interviewer(s)	Date of Publication in the HBR
17.	Paul Allaire	CEO	Xerox	Robert Howard	September–October 1992
18.	Tom Chapman	CEO	Greater Southeast Community Hospital	Nancy A. Nichols	November–December 1992
19.	Nicolas Hayek	CEO	Swiss Corporation for Microelectronics and Watchmaking (SMH)	William Taylor	March–April 1993
20.	Ernesto Martens	CEO	Vitro	Nancy A. Nichols	September–October 1993
21.	Edward McCracken	CEO	Silicon Graphics	Steven E. Prokesch	November–December 1993
22.	David Whitwam	CEO	Whirlpool	Regina Fazio Maruca	March–April 1994
23.	P. Roy Vagelos	CEO	Merck	Nancy A. Nichols	November–December 1994
24.	Lawrence Bossidy	CEO	Allied Signal	Noel Tichy and Ram Charan	March–April 1995
25.	John Sawhill	CEO	Nature Conservancy	Alice Howard and Joan Magretta	September–October 1995

26.	Sir Colin Marshall	Chairman and CEO	British Airways	Steven E. Prokesch	November–December 1995
27.	Robert Shapiro	CEO	Monsanto	Joan Magretta	January–February 1997
28.	John Browne	CEO	British Petroleum	Steven E. Prokesch	September–October 1997
29.	Krister Ahlstorm	CEO	Ahlstorm	Joan Magretta	January–February 1998
30.	Michael Dell	CEO	Dell Computers	Joan Magretta	March–April 1998
31.	Franco Bernabe	CEO	Eni	Linda Hill and Suzy Wetlaufer	July–August 1998
32.	Victor Fung	CEO	Li & Fung	Joan Magretta	September–October 1998
33.	Roger Sant and Dennis Bakke	Chairman and CEO, respectively	AES Corporation	Suzy Wetlaufer	January–February 1999
34.	Jacques Nasser	CEO	Ford	Suzy Wetlaufer	March–April 1999
35.	George Conrades	CEO	Akamai Technologies	Nicholas G. Carr	May–June 2000
36.	Andy Law	CEO	St. Luke's Communications	Diane L. Coutu	September–October 2000
37.	Michael Eisner	CEO	Walt Disney Co.	Suzy Wetlaufer	January–February 2000

Ford's knowledge sharing practices. In addition, a few in-depth case studies of the CEOs and their knowledge management roles in their organizations conducted by the author were used to corroborate the interviews. These case studies involved, among other things, detailed perusal and verification of information from multiple sources on these CEOs. This pattern of data verification through multiple sources was satisfactorily accomplished for all the interviews.

A detailed analysis of these interviews suggests that knowledge leaders engage in the building and maintenance of knowledge networks across the length and breadth of their organizations. They then utilize this knowledge network in managing knowledge including its creation, sharing, leveraging, and dissemination to appropriate destinations. In addition, successful knowledge leaders also engage in managing knowledge with external entities such as suppliers and customers (upstream and downstream in the value-chain) both through technological means and through social knowledge networks. The following sections are organized in this fashion. First, I discuss the aspect of knowledge networks (a component of Knowledge Management [KM]) implemented by the leaders and their impact on organizational performance. Then I discuss the concept of customer-focus and the role of knowledge management in focusing on customers. In both these areas, based on the activities of leaders in the 37 firms, practical propositions are developed and presented, based on the study findings. In each section, specific quotes from the CEOs (some of which are presented in the main text, the others presented in tables) that clearly express their personal views and their actions are presented. These tables and the quotes in them serve to illustrate Knowledge Leadership applications.

Knowledge Network

The presence of a knowledge network is a common occurrence in companies that are successful at knowledge and information management. Consistent with the approach of two different strategies for Knowledge Management–codification and personalization–the most important factor in managing knowledge is the way a company organizes its units and people. Thus, technological knowledge networks are not the only means to manage knowledge. The CEOs of the 37 firms used a range of knowledge networks from personalization to codification to a combination of both the approaches. Some quotations from the interviews are discussed in this section. Table 3.2 provides a broader sample of such quotes indicating the different types of knowledge networks in use. The quotes listed in the tables are just a representative sample of the broader evidence available for successful Knowledge Leadership practices available in these and other cases.

Table 3.2 identifies the various operational components of Knowledge Management as implemented by CEOs in their organizations. These operational components, identified earlier from current knowledge management wisdom, range from broad notions of socio-cognitive networks and technological networks to narrower components, such as councils, committees, teams, job rotation, appropriate organization structuring, internal and external benchmarking, selection, and training and development. For each of these operational components, Table 3.2 provides samples of quotes from the CEO interviews that illustrate their role in managing, sharing, and distributing knowledge in organizations.

Jacques Nasser of Ford uses the personalization approach to knowledge management by setting up elaborate networks of people who meet face to face and teach each other about the knowledge they have acquired. In Nasser's words, "We have to change our fundamental approach...our DNA. And teaching does that better than any other way I know." "Spreading knowledge is part of it (teaching). There is no better, faster way to distribute knowledge than through teaching" (Wetlaufer 1999).

Nasser's teaching initiative implemented at Ford consists of multiple programs at different levels (labeled variously as Capstone, Business Leadership Initiative, and Let's Chat About Business) in

Table 3.2

EXECUTIVE QUOTES PERTAINING TO KNOWLEDGE NETWORKS

CEO and Organization	Knowledge Leadership Aspect	Quotes from the Interviews
Jacques Nasser, Ford	Knowledge network, Socio-cognitive network	"Spreading knowledge is part of it (teaching). There is no better, faster way to distribute knowledge than through teaching."
Michael Dell, Dell Computer Corporation	Technological network	"We've developed customized intranet sites called premier pages for well over 200 of our largest global customers. . . . One of our customers, for example, allows its 50, 000 employees to view and select products online."
Jack Welch, General Electric	Councils, Committees, Internal benchmarking	"We also run a corporate executive council, the CEC. We share ideas and information candidly and openly, including programs that have failed." "Another of our jobs is transfer best practices across all the businesses, with lightning speed." "The ultimate objective of the work-out is clear. We want 300,000 people with different objectives and goals to share directly in the company's vision, the information, the decision making process, and the rewards."
Robert Haas, Levi Strauss	Technological network, Information sharing	"Our electronic data interchange system was a pioneering effort to communicate with our customers and manage the order replenishment cycle faster and more accurately." "We have established a company wide taskforce that's looking at how to balance work commitments."

Percy Barnevik, ABB	Job rotation, teams Organizational structure (socio-cognitive network)	"We rotate people around the world. There is no substitute for line experience in 3 or 4 countries to create a global perspective.... You also encourage people to work in mixed-nationality teams. You force them to create personal alliances across borders." "ABB is an organization with 3 internal contradictions. We want to be global and local, big and small, radically decentralized with centralized reporting and control.... That's where the matrix comes in..."
Alain Gomez, Thomson S.A.	Joint Ventures, Licensing agreement	"The trick is to learn from your competitors. Thompson consumer electronics has done that twice...RCA in picture tubes...with the Japanese in VCRs.... Less than 20 years ago we did not know how to produce picture tubes. Now we are among the leaders. We had to learn from RCA through a licensing agreement and a joint venture."
Paul Cook, Raychem	HR selection based on knowledge	"One of my most important jobs is finding the right people to add to the Raychem environment—people who genuinely want to serve the customer.... that means learning how their minds work, what they think about, what excites them, how they approach problems.... I spend 20% of my time recruiting, interviewing, training..."

(Table 3.2 continued)

(Table 3.2 continued)

CEO and Organization	Knowledge Leadership Aspect	Quotes from the Interviews
	Personalization/codification	"You also have to make sure your company has the very brightest people in your core technologies…you make sure these people talk to each other, that there is regular and intensive interchange between those disciplines. They have to work together, communicate, sweat, swear, and do whatever it takes to extract from the core technology every product possibility. The fax machine…absolutely magnificent…much more important than videoconferencing…we recently started a 'Not Invented Here' award at Raychem. We celebrate people who steal ideas from other parts of the company and apply them to their work."
Dennis Bakke, AES	Information sharing/ organizational memory	"There's the incredibly important matter of free and frequent information flow…it undergirds everything we do. When people are making big decisions on the front lines, it's not as if they are doing so in a vacuum. We have lots and lots of corporate memory, and it's crucial for people to be able to access it… all financial and market information is widely circulated. That's why for SEC purposes, every one of our people is considered an 'insider' for stock trading."
John Browne, British Petroleum	Leader attitude towards creating and distributing knowledge	"It is the key to being able to identify opportunities that others might not see and to exploit those opportunities rapidly and fully. This means that in order to generate extraordinary value for shareholders, a company has to learn better than its competitors and apply that knowledge throughout its businesses faster and more widely than they do. The way we see it, anyone in the organization who is not directly accountable for making a profit should be involved in creating and distributing knowledge that the company can use to make a profit."

David Whitwam, Whirlpool	Leader role in changing organizational structure	"The top management team must stimulate the organization, not control it. Its role is to provide strategic directives, to encourage learning, and to make sure there are mechanisms for transferring the lessons. The role of leaders at all levels is to demonstrate to people that they are capable of achieving more than they can achieve and that they should never be satisfied with where they are now." "You must create an organization whose people are adept at exchanging ideas, processes, and systems across borders, people who are absolutely free of the 'not-invented-here' syndrome, people who are constantly working together to identify the best global opportunities and the biggest global problems facing the organization."
Victor Fung, Li and Fung	Low technology and Socio-cognitive memory	"At one level, Li and Fung is an information node, flipping information between our 350 customers and our 7500 suppliers. We manage all that today with a lot of phone calls and faxes and on-site visits. Soon we will need a sophisticated information system with very open architecture to accommodate different protocols from different suppliers and from customers, one robust enough to work in Hong Kong and in New York—as well in places like Bangladesh, where you can't always count on a good phone line." "As the sources of supply explode, managing information becomes increasingly complex. Of course, we have a lot of hard data about performance and about the work we do with each factory. But what we really want is difficult to pin down, a lot of the most valuable information resides in people's heads. . . . That kind of organizational memory is a lot harder to retain and share. We see the capturing of such information as the next frontier."

(Table 3.2 continued)

(Table 3.2 continued)

CEO and Organization	Knowledge Leadership Aspect	Quotes from the Interviews
P. Roy Vagelos, Merck	Cross-functional teams	"No one has all the answers to business problems. When you work with knowledge professionals—experts in science, manufacturing, marketing, or administration—you are working with equals, people who excel in their disciplines. . . . Cross-functional interactions are crucial to drug development. It doesn't matter if the world's best biologists and chemists start the process—you must have the best people to carry it through every step of the way. The development process must be seamless or, I guarantee you, it will fail."
Lawrence A. Bossidy, Allied Signal	External benchmarking	"Benchmarking is not industrial tourism. It is looking at specific practices, getting the benefit of expertise, bringing it back, and having no inhibitions about adopting it and letting people know where it came from. . . . We bounce around depending on where we think the expertise is, and we benchmark many companies. For new product development, 3M has done a good job. For acquisitions, it might be Emerson Electric. In manufacturing and inventory management, we've looked at Motorola; and for receivables, American Express. I ask my senior managers to go to as many companies as they can, and I also do it myself."

the organization starting from the top with senior executives to the bottom with everyone who receives e-mail at Ford (about 100,000 employees). Thus, at Ford though the major focus is spreading knowledge through teaching, it is aided significantly through their e-mail network to which a large number of employees are connected.

At Dell, the success of their entire business model depends on the sophisticated data exchange enabled by the knowledge network that they have in place. Customers, suppliers, and employees are all connected to the knowledge network at Dell and use the network for different purposes (Magretta 1998). Dell uses its internet website and a number of customized intranet sites that provide access to various knowledge resources to customers, suppliers, and employees. In Dell's words:

> The technology available today really boosts the value of information sharing. We can share design databases and methodologies with supplier-partners in ways that just weren't possible five to ten years ago. This speeds time to market—often dramatically—and creates a lot of value that can be shared between buyer and supplier. (Magretta 1998)

At GE, Jack Welch operates on a simple belief that information sharing and knowledge sharing is crucial to the success of organizations. As with most other CEOs in this study, we found that this realization on the part of CEOs (leaders) that information sharing is crucial to their success was very instrumental in their development of knowledge sharing initiatives in their organizations. In Welch's words:

> You see, I operate on a very simple belief about business. If there are six of us in a room, and we all get the same facts, in most cases, the six of us will reach roughly the same conclusion...the problem is we don't get the same information. ...The complications arise when people are cut off from information they need. That's what we're trying to change. (Tichy and Ram Charan 1989)

At Merck, Roy Vagelos operates on a similar belief that led to Merck's acquisition of Medco, a prescription benefits management company. In Vagelos' words:

> Expanding our information base is critical to our achieving goals: Medco has data on 38 million patients, which allow us to learn a lot more about how our drugs are prescribed and used and, ultimately, how effective they are in fighting disease. Whether it is cutting edge scientific information or the reams of data on how doctors prescribe Merck products, information lies at the heart of what the company does. Our ability to leverage information will set us apart. (Nichols 1994)

In addition to the above, the idea that the CEOs as leaders of their organizations realize the importance of information and knowledge sharing is evident in the quotes of most CEOs in Table 3.2. The CEOs of Raychem (Paul Cook), AES (Dennis Bakke), British Petroleum (John Browne), Whirlpool (David Whitwam), and Li and Fung (Victor Fung) especially focus on the importance of knowledge sharing for organizational success. This realization of the importance of knowledge sharing is directly related to the actions and initiatives of these CEOs in the knowledge management realm, thus laying the foundation for organization-wide knowledge leadership.

The concept of knowledge network and its significance to the overall business model is consistently expressed by the CEOs of the leading companies chosen for this study. Thus, it leads us to the *Knowledge Leadership Propositions* that leaders recognize the value of knowledge management and realize the means through which knowledge can be managed. More importantly, all leaders use both technology and face-to-face participation in spreading knowledge to differing extents. Thus,

Knowledge Leadership Proposition 1: Leaders who realize the importance of knowledge management more than others lead their organizations to higher levels of performance.

Knowledge Leadership Proposition 2: Leaders who use technology and people more effectively in establishing knowledge networks and managing knowledge than others lead their organizations to higher levels of performance.

These two propositions, along with those related to customer-focused knowledge management, discussed next, are encapsulated in Figure 3.1, which presents a summary of the Knowledge Leadership model.

Figure 3.1
KNOWLEDGE LEADERSHIP MODEL

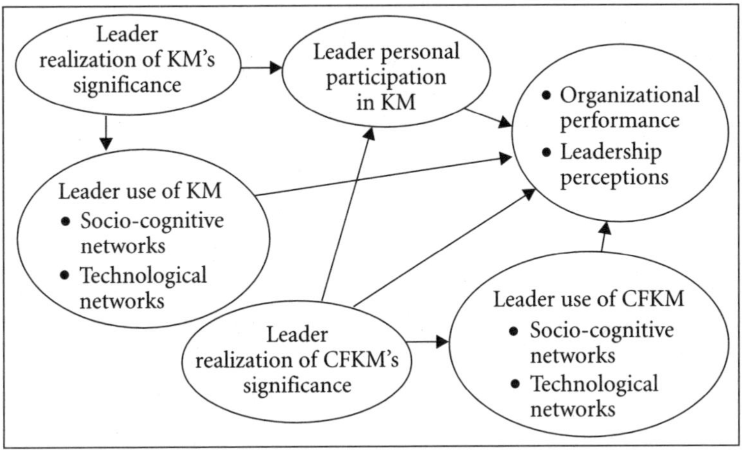

Notes: KM: Knowledge Management
CFKM: Customer-Focused Knowledge Management

Customer-Focused Knowledge Management

Knowledge Management across organizational boundaries has not been part of the discussion in the state-of-the-art Knowledge Management scholarship until recently, and therefore has not been adequately explored. Consonant with the notion that organizations can institute knowledge management processes with partners outside traditional organizational boundaries such as customers and suppliers, I found that the more successful CEOs expressed an attitude of intense customer-focus and realized the value of sharing knowledge and information vis-à-vis their customers.

The role of leaders in utilizing information management for better focusing on customers is highlighted by the CEOs in this study. Credible sources report that John Reed of Citibank traveled more than 400,000 miles per year—visiting customers, cajoling employees, and sizing up markets. John Reed explains the travel aspect of the knowledge sharing about customers in the global consumer banking business as follows:

> We started the consumer bank in 1974.... We flew to Belgium and all around Europe...London...Hong Kong...all around Asia...South America.... At each stop we studied what Citibank was doing, what was relevant to the consumer business, and how it could become part of a new business collective.... We made an important discovery...there were more similarities than differences among customers around the world. (Tichy and Ram Charan 1990)

The interview with Nasser highlights the importance of internal customers and the role of the leader in managing information to and from these internal customers. The "Let's chat about business" program, which is part of the overall organizational teaching initiative, is a crucial means through which Nasser shares information with everyone in the organization that receives e-mail. These e-mails go out every Friday at 5.00 p.m. Nasser describes this program as follows: "They're just another way to share the information—unfiltered—as broadly as possible throughout the company and to encourage dialogue at all levels" (Wetlaufer 1999).

Another aspect of the focus on internal customers at the executive level comes from the following Nasser quote:

> A few years ago, I started meeting with small groups of senior executives to talk about shareholder value and what that means in the daily approach to our jobs. The first few times, I spent hours talking about financial ratios. But it wasn't until someone was brave enough to come up to me and say, "What's a P/E ratio?" that I realized why so few people in the company were thinking about shareholder value. (Wetlaufer 1999)

This experience led to the development of a whole new program to educate employees in the organization about various issues including shareholder value. This is a direct result of sharing information with them.

At Dell, some of their clients have a dedicated on-site team of Dell employees that collect information and pass it back on to the organization. Dell's qualitative approach to sales forecasting includes a Dell executive walking through their customer's sites and obtaining information about their likely future requirements. This information is then built into their sales and demand forecasts. Dell also organizes what are called Platinum Council Meetings, which are regional meetings in which company executives share information with customers on a whole range of issues. In Michael Dell's words, "All of our senior executives participate in these meetings with our largest customers. The ratio is about one Dell person to one customer" (Magretta 1998).

> I spend three days at each of them (platinum council meetings). They're great events. In the normal course of our business, I have lots of opportunities to talk to customers one on one, but there is something much more powerful about this kind of forum. Customers tend to speak much more openly when they're with their peers and they know we're there and listening. (Magretta 1998)

At Silicon Graphics, Ed McCracken expresses a very strong belief in the importance of focusing on customers and sharing information with them, for everyone in the organization, especially their engineers and technologists. Such belief guides him in his efforts at instituting processes focused on enhancing such sharing of information with customers as well as internal organizational processes that would reward and appreciate such sharing of information. In McCracken's words:

> We encourage our first- and second-level engineering managers to spend time with customers. We rate our key managers every six months. I remember sitting in on an evaluation for engineering managers at which we lowered the rating of two or three because we thought that they and their teams hadn't spent enough time with customers.... Our division managers aren't there to manage our financial performance. Their job is to manage a special relationship between the technology and the customers' requirements. (Prokesch 1993)

These and many other CEOs, in the set of 37, personally emphasize the importance of both external and internal customers and the importance of the information that can be obtained from these events or activities. Table 3.3 provides a broader sample of quotes and indicates that the activities of the CEOs focused on managing knowledge vis-à-vis customers. The data in Table 3.3 indicates that most of these CEOs realized the importance of managing knowledge vis-à-vis customers, communicated this attitude clearly to their organizational members, and established organizational processes to manage such customer-focused knowledge. As in Table 3.2, Table 3.3 captures the different operational components of customer-focused knowledge management, such as customer meets, traveling to meet customers, technological networks with customers, internal organizational processes tuned to customers, organizational structuring, customer-focused teams, customer-focused divisions, acquisitions to enhance such information sharing, and cross-functional teams that include customers. As in the case of knowledge networks, the quotes in the table are just a tip of the broader iceberg of the evidence available on customer-focused knowledge management.

Thus, this data led me to the conclusion that leaders take personal interest in using information and knowledge management to enhance the process of focusing on customers and obtaining valuable information in the process. Accordingly, the following Knowledge Leadership Propositions can be stated:

Knowledge Leadership Proposition 3: Leaders who understand the role and significance of knowledge management in providing and obtaining (sharing) information with customers (internal and external) better than others lead their organizations to higher levels of performance.

Knowledge Leadership Proposition 4: Leaders who provide opportunities to all employees to obtain information from customers (internal and external) by using information networks in a better manner than others lead their organizations to higher levels of performance.

Table 3.3

EXECUTIVE QUOTES PERTAINING TO CUSTOMER-FOCUSED KNOWLEDGE SHARING

CEO and Organization	Knowledge Leadership Aspect	Quotes from the Interviews
Jacques Nasser, Ford	Internal customers	"A few years ago, I started meeting with small groups of senior executives to talk about shareholder value and what that means in the daily approach to our jobs. The first few times, I spent hours talking about financial ratios. But it wasn't until someone was brave enough to come up to me and say, 'What's a P/E ratio?' that I realized why so few people in the company were thinking about shareholder value."
Michael Dell, Dell Computer Corporation	Customer meets	"I spend three days at each of them (Platinum Council Meetings). They're great events. In the normal course of our business, I have lots of opportunities to talk to customers one on one, but there is something much more powerful about this kind of forum. Customers tend to speak much more openly when they're with their peers and they know we're there and listening."
John Reed, Citicorp	Traveling to meet customers	"We started the consumer bank in 1974…. We flew to Belgium and all around Europe…London…Hong Kong…all around Asia…South America…. At each stop we studied what Citibank was doing, what was relevant to the consumer business, and how it could become part of a new business collective…. We made an important discovery…there were more similarities than differences among customers around the world."
Robert Haas, Levi Strauss	Technological network for sharing knowledge with customers	"Our electronic data interchange system was a pioneering effort to communicate with our customers and manage the order replenishment cycle faster and more accurately."

(Table 3.3 continued)

(Table 3.3 continued)

CEO and Organization	Knowledge Leadership Aspect	Quotes from the Interviews
Lee Brown, New York City Police Commissioner	Using people and technology to share knowledge with customers (community policing)	"We had an officer who tried community policing in a neighborhood. He pulled people together so successfully that they even gave their neighborhood a name. In this area there was a rash of break-ins where the burglars were armed and showed no hesitancy to shoot. Under traditional policing, the neighborhood would have blamed the police. Instead the community organized itself. Flyers were handed our describing the pattern of the crimes. One citizen called in and we caught the burglars."
Sir Colin Marshall, British Airways	Internal organizational process tuned to customers	"…creating an organization that excels in listening to its most valuable customers. By creating data that enable you to measure the kinds of performance that create value for your customers…in several key places in our organization, we have created customer advocates…" "Our senior managers, myself included, consciously try to talk to a lot of our passengers…we also conduct customer forums…we ask our customers to let their imagination, anger, enthusiasm, and ideas flow so we can capture their thoughts about current as well as emergent issues."
George Fisher, Motorola	Changing organizational structure	"Here's the question we're wrestling with—How do we get people inside Motorola who know the customer best to have greater power? Our answer is to develop a management system that essentially flips the organization—a system that empowers the sales force…. Members of our sales force are surrogates of our customers. They should be able to reach back into Motorola and pull out technologists and other people they need to solve problems and anticipate customer needs. We want to put the salesperson at the top of the organization."

	Customer visits	"We've established a massive program of increasing customer visits at all levels of the organization. We want everyone in Motorola from top to bottom to go out and see customers and understand their business better. We did a survey on customer visits…not enough of our top-level people were making these visits. So Bob Galvin, our chairman, pushed people at the top of the company to get more involved with customers. He personally went out and made 10 or 12 customer visits, and he wrote extensive trip reports on each one."
Ed McCracken, Silicon Graphics	Customer-focused teams	"At Silicon Graphics, top management's role is to make sure that the company's organizational structure encourages our brightest technologists to maintain close working relationships with customers. Top management's role is to divide customers into segments determined by their needs and the technology required to satisfy them. Then we put a project team in each segment and let those teams decide what to design in cooperation with their customers. As long as the teams have bright ideas and are really excited about them, our top managers stay out of the way." "A company can't use traditional market research to pick up on paradigm shifts. Its best technologists, its most creative R and D people, must be out there to sense firsthand what its most creative customers—what we call our 'lighthouse' customers—might want in the future. These technologists aren't getting customer input on the current product line; they're getting some feeling about how they might define a brand-new product that would do things differently."

(Table 3.3 continued)

(*Table 3.3 continued*)

CEO and Organization	Knowledge Leadership Aspect	Quotes from the Interviews
Victor Fung, Li and Fung	Customer-focused divisions	"Customer-focused divisions are the building blocks of our organization. … Consider our Gymboree division, one of our largest. The division manager, Ada Liu, and her headquarters team have their own separate office space within the Li & Fung building in Hong Kong. When you walk through their door, every one of the 40 or so people you see is focused solely on meeting Gymboree's needs. On every desk is a computer with direct software links to Gymboree. The staff is organized into specialized teams in such areas as technical support, merchandising, raw material purchasing, quality assurance, and shipping. And Ada has dedicated sourcing teams in our branch offices in China, the Philippines, and Indonesia because Gymboree buys in volume from all those countries. In maybe 5 of our 26 countries, she has her own team, people she hired herself. When she wants to source from, say, India, the branch office helps her get the job done."
P. Roy Vagelos, Merck	Acquisition (Medco) to increase customer information sharing	"Our goal is to maximize the effectiveness of our drugs. First, we must develop the safest and most effective drugs possible in the labs. Then, once the drug is on the market and has been prescribed to a patient, we must be sure that the patient is taking the right drug, that he or she has the appropriate information to take the drug properly, and that the drug will not interfere with other medications the patient is taking. We can ensure all this by capturing information as it comes through the pharmacy and then putting it into a central data bank that feeds the information back to the physician, the plan sponsor, and ultimately the labs, where it can be used to create new drugs."

| Lawrence A. Bossidy, Allied Signal | Cross-functional teams including customers | "One danger, of course, is that scientists and managers may become overwhelmed by all this information and the possibilities it presents. At Merck, we must be able to condense reams of information and let our best judgment, not our worst fears prevail."

"So we said, 'Okay, we're going to do something about this.' And we went to the customers and said, 'Hey, we have a lot of problems, and we'd like to have your team with us so we can get them identified and solved.' Almost to a customer, they agreed to do that. We now have hundreds of multifunctional teams in place, and they have helped give our customers higher-quality products and faster turnaround time. ... The benefits of the teams go beyond solving specific problems. People often underestimate the importance of having face time with customers." |

Personal Knowledge Leadership of Executives

Personal participation by CEOs in knowledge management activities is perhaps the most crucial link between Knowledge Management and Leadership, giving rise to the notion of Organizational Knowledge Leadership. There is a consistent pattern in all of these CEO responses (verified by other sources) that the more successful CEOs personally participated in the knowledge management activities that they were very instrumental in establishing these ideas. The pattern also indicated that the establishment of these activities and then personal participation in them were a direct result of their personal realization of the significance of Knowledge Management to furthering organizational goals.

Talking about the *work-out* process he implemented at GE, Jack Welch indicates his passion and personal interest in the process and explains why he actively participates in numerous *work-out* sessions throughout the organization. In his own words:

> The ultimate objective of the work-out is so clear. We want 300,000 people with different career objectives, different family aspirations, different financial goals, to share directly in the company's vision, the information, the decision making process, and the rewards.... In 1989, the CEO is going to every business in this company to sit in on a work-out session. That's a little puzzling to them. "I own the business, what are you doing here?" they say. Well, I'm not there to tell them how to price products, what type of equipment they need, whom to hire; I have no comments on that.... But work-out is the next generation of what we're trying to do. We had to put in a process to focus on and change how work gets done in this company. We have to apply the same relentless passion to work-out that we did in selling the vision of number one and number two globally. That's why we're pushing it so hard, getting so involved. (Tichy and Charan 1989)

Michael Dell talks about the value of personal participation in the forums set up to ensure free flow of information with customers on a constant basis such as the Platinum Councils, regional meetings of Dell's largest customers in Asia-Pacific, Japan, the United States, and Europe.

All of our senior executives from around the company participate, spending time with the customer, listening to how we're doing. The ratio is about one Dell person to one customer. At our last session, we had about 100 customers.... I spend three days at each of them (Platinum Council meetings). They're great events. In the normal course of business, I have lots of opportunity to talk to customers one on one, but there is something more powerful about this kind of forum. Customers tend to speak more openly when they're with peers and they know we're there and we're listening. (Magretta 1998)

At Allied Signal, Lawrence Bossidy participates in information sharing both internally with employees, and externally with customers, thereby encouraging others in the organization and reinforcing the value of the forums instituted for such purposes.

First, we want to create an environment in which people will speak up. Every question is interesting and important. When I conduct interactive sessions, I don't walk out after three questions. I make it clear that I'm going to be there until the last question is asked. When employees point out things that aren't right, I'm the first to say, "Yes, that's one we need to do something about, and here's what we're going to do". Or, "I don't know the answer to that, but I'll look into it"—and then I'd better follow up. (Tichy and Charan 1995)

I made an effort to talk to customers early on, but that's something you need to do all the time, not just in the first 60 days. I visited a lot of customers, and in my first few months I really got an earful. I tried to get examples in every sector—and I still do. (Tichy and Charan 1995)

At Silicon Graphics, Ed McCracken talks about the process through which they ensure that their engineering managers actually participate in forums of information sharing with customers, and his personal participation in such processes.

We encourage our first- and second-level engineering managers to spend time with customers. We rate our key managers every six months. I remember sitting in on an evaluation for engineering managers at which we lowered the rating of two or three because we thought that they and their teams hadn't spent enough time with customers. Our division managers aren't there to manage our financial performance. Their job is to manage a special relationship between the technology and the customer's requirements. (Prokesch 1993)

Thus, from a behavioral perspective, by personally participating both on a day-to-day basis and in specially organized events, in information sharing, these CEOs send valuable signals to all those concerned about the importance of the information that can be obtained through such knowledge networks.

Accordingly,

Knowledge Leadership Proposition 5: Leaders who personally participate in the process of sharing information in day-to-day activities and specially organized information networks to a larger extent than others lead their organizations to higher levels of performance.

The findings of this multiple-case analysis suggest that leaders are acutely aware of the role of information and knowledge sharing and design knowledge networks that serve to maximize organizational effectiveness. Moreover, leaders use information technology and knowledge management to better focus on key internal and external customers. Thus, this suggests that both the leader behavior dimensions of information search and acquisition, and information use in problem solving identified earlier by experts are also crucial in Knowledge Leadership. More importantly, the comparative analysis of CEO interviews conducted by different interviewers links the processes of knowledge management and customer-focused knowledge management to leader effectiveness and organizational effectiveness. Rich case information of how, when, and by what means these top executives engaged in knowledge leadership is likely to be very fruitful for the readers of this book.

The evidence presented from the interviews as shown in the quotes is consistent with other portions of the interviews and are only meant to be a representative sample. The complete interviews and the cross-section of interviews provide broader evidence of the Knowledge Leadership phenomenon. The rest of this book focuses on some of the dimensions of this broader phenomenon of Knowledge Leadership.

As indicated in the Knowledge Leadership model (Figure 3.1), the leader's role in knowledge management starts with the leader's own realization of the importance of information and knowledge management to the effective performance of the organization. More specifically, such realization of the importance of knowledge management needs to manifest itself along two dimensions, one internal and the other external. Internally, the leader's realization of the importance of knowledge management is instrumental in the leader's establishment of both technological and socio-cognitive routes for managing knowledge in their organizations. Externally, the leader's realization of the importance of customer-focused knowledge management is instrumental in the leader's establishment of both technological and socio-cognitive routes for managing such knowledge. Other external targets/sources for knowledge management also exist, such as suppliers, investors, regulators, and employee groups. Supplier-focused knowledge management initiatives in the Brazilian Automobile industry are detailed in a subsequent chapter. As indicated in the relevant tables, this comparative analysis approach highlights the different operational (practical) indicators of each of these routes for managing knowledge as established by the CEOs of the organizations included in the study. The practical components for Knowledge Management are drawn from current knowledge management wisdom. This study makes an important contribution by making special emphasis on the new approaches to leadership in the 21st century and identifying leadership imperatives under the new rules of business.

NOTE

1. For more details on the scientific approach, see Lakshman (2007a).

4

MICRO-KNOWLEDGE LEADERSHIP

LEADERSHIP FOR ALL MANAGERS

> *You also have to make sure your company has the very brightest people in your core technologies...you make sure these people talk to each other, that there is regular and intensive interchange between those disciplines. They have to work together, communicate, sweat, swear, and do whatever it takes to extract from the core technology every product possibility. The fax machine...absolutely magnificent...much more important than videoconferencing...we recently started a "Not Invented Here" award at Raychem. We celebrate people who steal ideas from other parts of the company and apply them to their work.*
>
> —Paul Cook, Raychem
> (In an interview with William Taylor, *HBR*, 1990)

Shifting our focus from top executives to managers lower down in the organization, this chapter focuses on micro-level concepts of Knowledge Leadership as opposed to the macro-level concept discussed in the previous chapter. All managers are entrusted with the responsibility of leading the different groups in their units or departments/divisions. These may be multiple groups or just one large group of individuals. Regardless, as in conventional leadership approaches, the fundamental task of the manager is to provide leadership to these groups of individuals. Such leadership is primarily at an interpersonal level. As detailed in one of the introductory chapters, managers should pay attention to their attributes, personality traits, behaviors, and leadership style preferences for influencing these groups at both interpersonal and group levels and lead them to higher achievements. In the radically new knowledge economy, however, such straight leadership may hardly be sufficient to achieve a competitive edge. It is necessary to infuse knowledge leadership at the interpersonal level of leadership as well. Managers desirous of providing knowledge leadership to their units should focus on the following ideas to achieve excellence in this new economic context.

1. First and foremost, managers have to examine their knowledge base in the form of cause-effect beliefs and continuously refine these beliefs to the point that subordinates, peers, and superiors see these beliefs as reasonable and acceptable. Leadership experts suggest that these chains of cause-effect beliefs are of utmost importance for leaders to emerge from the bowels of the organization and move onto higher levels of leadership responsibility. Thus, knowledge of the business and the associated processes is the predominant precursor to successful knowledge leadership.

2. Managers intending to provide knowledge leadership should focus on their information search and acquisition behaviors and improve these to fairly high levels. Managers have to

act like and become information junkies so that they can be considered by others as information storehouses. This requires the fundamental realization that information is at the heart of decision-making and that the quality of such decision-making rapidly increases in the presence of such information.

3. Having searched and acquired the information, managers need to focus on their actions that will make use of this information in problem solving. This will send signals to others in the organization that the manager makes decisions based on the appropriate information and is skilled in such processes. This improves managerial credibility to remarkable levels, compared to those who do not rely on appropriate information in decision-making.

4. To realize both of the aforementioned aims, managers need to establish channels of information and knowledge flow, in addition to creation of the right climate for information flows. The climate established in the unit should provide sufficient levels of comfort to others to openly share information, or alternatively provide sufficient reinforcement (incentives) to share the information that they possess.

5. To create the right climate within their units, managers need to focus their efforts and their influence skills on populating their units with the appropriate specialists. Engaging with peers and superiors and influencing them about the appropriate expertise bases required in the unit is an essential task of such knowledge leaders. Knowledge leaders have to create and develop their own expertise base and become acknowledged experts in their chosen domain. The knowledge leader's job is to also to ensure that the responsibilities of people in their units match their expertise. To foster this climate further, it is imperative that knowledge leaders know who the experts are in their units and make everyone else in the unit aware of the different experts available within the

unit. Creating trust in the minds of everyone in the unit on the expertise bases of the individuals is another crucial task, which will make people place trust and faith and thus gain comfort from such experts' analyses and suggestions.

6. The knowledge leader should build mini-learning communities within their units to reflect those at higher levels in their organization. These should serve as conduits for processes that convert information into knowledge, and tacit knowledge into explicit knowledge, thus making it easy to be transferred from one place to another. The knowledge leader needs to remember that information does not get converted into knowledge in the absence of processes (such as the learning communities) that make it happen.

7. Finally, the knowledge leader needs to serve as a role model and lead by example, in building one's own knowledge base and in terms of using the information and knowledge channels, to actively transfer content and disseminate them to where they are required. These knowledge leader imperatives and the framework to organize these ideas are described in detail in this chapter.

MICRO-LEVEL KNOWLEDGE LEADERSHIP

There are plenty of similarities in knowledge leadership at the executive level and at all other managerial levels. It is a different matter altogether that the knowledge leadership at executive levels is also different in a number of ways and that these two components are not entirely isomorphic. However, the keen reader will quickly latch on to the similarities in the concept across levels. A simple model of Knowledge Leadership is provided in Figure 4.1. The figure suggests that the leader's knowledge about business and specifically cause-effect beliefs is an important precursor to effective knowledge leadership. This model also includes leader behaviors

Figure 4.1

KNOWLEDGE LEADERSHIP FOR MANAGERS AT ALL LEVELS

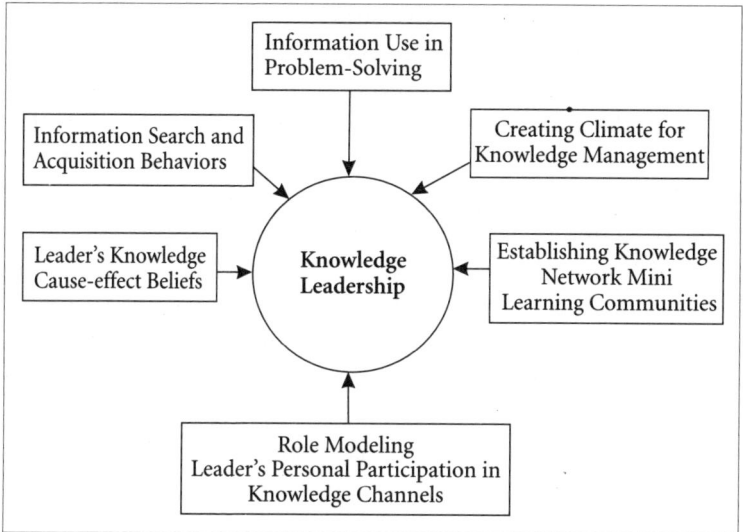

of information search and acquisition, information use in problem solving, creating a climate for managing knowledge, establishing networks for knowledge flows, and perhaps most importantly, leader role modeling of attitudes and behaviors towards knowledge creation, sharing, leveraging, and dissemination.

The figure and the Knowledge Leadership imperatives it suggests are explained in detail in the following pages. The inherent focus in this chapter is on an individual's traits, other characteristics, behaviors, and actions that provide effective knowledge leadership to their units and subsequently to their organizations.

Cause-Effect Beliefs

Organizational and strategic management experts have examined the impact of managerial cognitive structures and perceptions on organizational performance. In the context of a model of leadership and information processing, some experts suggest that the cognitive structures of managers can provide a basis for decision-making. They argue that these cognitive structures provide the managers with the "metastrategies" for decision-making and that these can be thought of as the "implicit theories" of managers.

One leadership expert who is commonly associated with the field of transformational leadership is James Burns (Burns 1978). While addressing the topic of leadership and decision-making, he emphasized the crucial importance of a leader's understanding of past and future decisions and their consequences for achieving organizational objectives. Emphasizing the complexity surrounding managerial decision-making, Burns stressed on the role of a decision maker's calculations on how to use and adapt chains of cause and effect relevant to their goals. This expert suggested that leaders must anticipate how various groups and the public would react to different decisions and modify their own actions accordingly. He further emphasized the importance of an understanding on the part of leaders—past decisions and their consequences, and anticipation of future decisions and their consequences. Burns' work suggested that leaders need to possess knowledge in the form of cause-effect beliefs and that they need to learn from both the past and the present in the continuous formation and refining of their "implicit theories."

The ambiguity surrounding executive decisions and their uncertain acceptability on the part of subordinates necessitates that managers have clarity and substantiation for their belief structures for these to be effectively understood and accepted by others in organizations. This is all the more important because the nature of pluralistic societies is such that the stream of cause and effect is shifting and multi-channeled. Other experts note that the completeness of cause-effect beliefs and the clarity with which these are held, hold important consequences for attaining organizational effectiveness. Knowledge in the field of social psychology suggests that the stability of individuals' beliefs are likely to be important in obtaining acceptance and consensus that are crucial for implementation of key decisions. Group pressures on individual beliefs have very little impact on the stability of those beliefs when the individual has empirical confirmation for them readily at hand. When such empirical anchorage is lacking, the stability of those beliefs is also lacking due to group pressures. In the context of the trait approach to leadership, which suggests that self-confidence on the part of leaders is of crucial importance to effectiveness, it is noted here that confidence and clarity or firmness in the beliefs held by executive leaders is very important for organizations and their units to achieve effectiveness, through the implementation of decisions that follow from the cause-effect beliefs. Thus, the primary task of the knowledge leader is to refine their implicit theories by examining their own personal experiences and learning from vicarious experiences of their role models.

Informational Role

Leadership experts have also identified the informational role played by managers as one of the crucial roles in organizations (Minzberg 1973). The informational role is the one that has most relevance for the knowledge leader. The knowledge leader plays this role by exhibiting behaviors such as information search and acquisition, and information use in problem solving. The knowledge leader needs to become an information junkie to play this role to perfection. It is imperative that knowledge leaders cultivate their own sources of information among relatively low-ranking subordinates, unconstrained by the organizational structure. The central objective is to create a network of information that can provide highly reliable and accurate real-time information and knowledge. This may involve changing or modifying the organizational structure locally rather than organization wide. By cultivating such a network, the knowledge leader will have accomplished the exhibiting of information search and acquisition, and information use in problem solving behaviors. Further, the knowledge leader should engage his/her subordinates in discussion and debate so that they are ready to answer tough questions and ensure that plans and their implementation do not falter. Engaging in this discussion and debate requires the behavior of information use in problem solving not only on the part of the knowledge leader but also on the part of his/her subordinates.

Creating Climate for Knowledge Management

Knowledge Leadership experts suggest that one of the key behaviors required for successfully inculcating knowledge management practices in organizational units is creation of a climate that is ripe for such objectives. Creating mutual trust in the minds of all the subordinates is of primary importance in this regard. This trust needs to manifest itself in terms of the faith placed in specialists and their expertise bases, their analysis and suggestions, and the use of these in decision-making. In order to ensure that this happens, the knowledge leader needs to move up and down the vertical channel, and sideways in the horizontal organizational channel influencing and eliciting support for populating the unit with the requisite levels of expertise. These attempts need to focus on bringing in only the best and brightest individuals in each domain. Establishing a climate of mutual trust is likely to be very difficult without these efforts. The knowledge leader should familiarize himself/herself with the experts in each unit and their corresponding specializations. The ultimate objective of the knowledge leader is to make everyone in the unit aware of the experts and their respective specializations so that it is easy for people to turn to the appropriate person in a time of need and use them in solving their problem with high-levels of trust, confidence, and faith in their judgment.

Successful knowledge leaders also have to infuse systems thinking in the minds of these subordinates and work constantly towards the development of their skills and expertise. Systems thinking involves the ability to conceive of the interdependent sets of cause-effect streams in the multiple units within the organization and to a certain extent outside of it. As suggested by leadership experts, cause-effect chains in today's knowledge economy are varied and multi-channeled. Thus, each unit's actions are likely to have ripple effects and other types of consequences on other units' actions. Anticipating these cause-effect chains is a critical component of systems thinking; fostering these is the knowledge leader's responsibility. Establishing creative tension through the debates and discussions, while exhibiting the knowledge leader's own knowledge of systemic effects, is one way of fostering such systems thinking, in addition to the basic objective of using information in problem solving, pursuant to its search and acquisition.

Establishing Knowledge Network

Establishing a knowledge network in the absence of the right climate would be fruitless and frustrating, contributing to the failure of knowledge leadership experienced by quite a few organizations and managers within them. The establishment of the knowledge network should build on the sources of information, uniquely cultivated by the leader, alluded to earlier. Knowledge is nothing but information placed in its context to be made sense of, thus reflecting some amount of processing by multiple individuals in the form of teams or learning communities. Thus, knowledge leaders need to possess this basic realization that information has to be put through some processes before it becomes useful knowledge that can then be codified and disseminated to where it is needed. *Socialization* processes in teams, discussion groups, learning communities, mini-conferences, and meetings accomplish this objective of converting information to knowledge. It is the knowledge leader's responsibility therefore to establish such socialization processes in their units.

Arranging for common discussions (having populated the unit with experts that everyone can identify and place trust in), forming task forces and committees, or other online discussion groups and learning communities are the perfect means to fulfill such responsibilities. Today's technology tools, such as mobile phones, voice-mail networks, e-mail groups, and other online discussion groups facilitate the establishment of such knowledge networks. Old-fashioned fax machines and telephones could also be utilized to serve this purpose. Organizational support, if needed, is also to be obtained by exerting influence vertically and horizontally in the hierarchy. Both socialization and technology-based processes can and should be utilized for this purpose. Effective knowledge leaders will harness these processes to maximum benefit within their units and serve as an exemplar for other units in their organizations.

Role Modeling

Nothing is as effective in leadership as that which is achieved by "leadership by example." This is the critical realization, based on which the Knowledge Leadership model identified here and by other Knowledge Leadership experts identify the importance of role modeling values, attitudes, and behaviors by the leader. Knowledge leaders should first and foremost set an example with their own knowledge and attitudes towards expanding its base. Being open to feedback and new learning is one way to exhibit the right attitude towards new knowledge acquisition. Knowledge leaders should role model their cause-effect beliefs by constantly espousing them and thereby exhibiting their complexity and comprehensiveness. Setting an example in this regard is critical for knowledge leaders, who should set standards for others to meet. Extensive and active participation in the knowledge network established would also serve to send signals to all concerned about the importance of knowledge sharing and thus be more effective in eliciting participation on the part of the key sources of information. These signals would also indicate the knowledge leader's commitment to the whole process of creating, sharing, leveraging, and disseminating knowledge. Such perception of the leader's commitment goes a long way in encouraging others to fully engage in these activities in the knowledge domain. Such role modeling can also be backed up by appropriate incentives and remuneration for encouraging knowledge domain activities, which further intensifies the commitment of the knowledge leaders.

In addition to all of the aforementioned dimensions of Knowledge Leadership, building personal rapport and strong relationships with all subordinates, based on personal knowledge of each of them, greatly enhances the human touch that knowledge leaders bring to the table. Of course, it goes without saying that personal knowledge-based rapport building is only possible in the presence of a strong caring attitude towards the individuals concerned and the basic valuing of relationships in managing work accomplishments. This is especially true of knowledge leaders with a fairly large span of people under their control. In this context, remembering the scores of subordinates by name, personal details, and their specializations would all serve to signify the importance attached to the individuals concerned and therefore garner higher levels of commitment from them. Other leadership attributes, over and above those identified earlier, such as resolving conflicts in the learning communities, ensuring smooth flow of processes, reducing confusion about processes, and enhancing coordination levels among the subordinates would all help in maximizing the benefits of knowledge leadership.

Organizations can only harness knowledge when a significant number of its constituent units are engaged in effectively harnessing knowledge. There is a certain 'critical mass' effect to these kinds of activities, which requires sufficient numbers of managers to engage in knowledge leadership. Knowledge leaders stand to benefit from such contributions to their organizations by enhancing their own credibility, managerial reputation, subordinate support and satisfaction, leadership effectiveness, and the potential of an enhanced career, one with high-levels of leadership responsibilities at increasingly higher levels in the organization. Not engaging in knowledge leadership, of course, has its consequences of being out of tune with the economic and environmental context within which business operates in today. This has severe consequences for one's own managerial effectiveness and reputation. Managerial reputation, it turns out, is a significant currency on which rests the potential of leadership. The choices are clear for managers in this new economic environment. Organizations and their top managers would do well to encourage their lower level managers to make the right choices along the way.

5

CUSTOMER-FOCUSED KNOWLEDGE LEADERSHIP

MICHAEL DELL

...creating an organization that excels in listening to its most valuable customers. By creating data that enable you to measure the kinds of performance that create value for your customers...in several key places in our organization, we have created customer advocates.... Our senior managers, myself included, consciously try to talk to a lot of our passengers...we also conduct customer forums...we ask our customers to let their imagination, anger, enthusiasm, and ideas flow so we can capture their thoughts about current as well as emergent issues.

—**Sir Colin Marshall, British Airways**
(In an interview with S.E. Prokesch, *HBR*, 1995)

Managing the value-chain has gained significant prominence in recent years. Top executives and other strategic managers of the world's leading corporations have become all too familiar with the concepts of value-chain management. Key strategies are developed by analyzing value-chains to achieve higher levels of efficiency and effectiveness in multiple parts of the value-chain. Many companies including Dell Computers have attempted strategies such as vertical integration, either backward into the upstream businesses or downstream into the distribution of products and services. Many other companies also assess the profit margin generation from activities in different parts of the value-chain and choose to exit low margin activities and focus on only the high margin ones. Some others also focus on operational processes among business activities in different parts of the value-chain and reengineer them to achieve quicker and more efficient delivery of outputs to the market. However, very few companies engage in knowledge leadership across the value-chain to establish a strong competitive edge and an unbreakable hold on the market places they operate in. Dell Inc. is an example of such a company engaging in sharing and leveraging knowledge vis-à-vis both suppliers on the upstream side of the value-chain and customers on the downstream side of the value-chain. The supplier-focused and customer-focused knowledge management has given such an edge to Dell that is unimaginable, given the degree to which they are above par vis-à-vis their competition in the personal computer business. This chapter provides a case study of Dell's supplier-focused and customer-focused knowledge management under Michael Dell's knowledge leadership to highlight the significance of these practices for sustained competitive advantage. Using evidence from qualitative, archival, and interview data, this chapter suggests that supplier-focused knowledge management and customer-focused knowledge management are powerful tools in terms of the impact of such knowledge management on organizational performance. More importantly, the role of executive leaders in knowledge management along both of these dimensions is critical to harnessing these powerful tools. The evidence from this case study suggests the importance of these types of Knowledge Management for practitioners and academics alike.

Recently, experts in Knowledge Management have stressed the need for more in-depth investigation of the concept. For instance, these experts call for more study on the relatively rare investigations of knowledge management across organizational boundaries. Such knowledge management across organizational boundaries can be with suppliers and/or customers among other external entities, as suggested by the Dell Inc. case study.

The study described in this chapter combines the two expert suggestions by focusing this investigation on the role leaders play in two broad dimensions of Knowledge Management, namely, supplier-focused knowledge management and customer-focused knowledge management. Drawing from the Knowledge Management and Leadership literatures, I identify the knowledge management activities of a top executive leader (namely, Michael Dell) that are simultaneously focused on suppliers and customers. Drawing from a variety of archival sources of information on Dell Inc., I provide evidence to suggest that Dell derives its competitive advantage in the computer industry by virtue of its customer-focused knowledge management and supplier-focused Knowledge Management. Drawing specifically from interviews of Michael Dell, I suggest that this entrepreneurially driven company exemplifies leadership focused on both of these sub-components of Knowledge Management.

Having read through the previous chapter on knowledge leadership at lower levels in the organization (micro-knowledge leadership), readers need to be reminded that although the current state of knowledge on leadership focusing on the functions of top managers has identified and emphasized the importance of the informational role of top managers, and the importance of information to create a vision, it has not focused on the management of information or the management of knowledge as key leadership roles. Additionally, as described earlier, although some experts have focused on leader behavior descriptions such as information search and acquisition, and information use in problem solving, this work remains at a nascent stage and has not been developed further. Other experts have identified the design and building of information systems as a key leader activity leading to improved organizational performance. This chapter builds on the basics of Knowledge Leadership described in the previous chapters and digs deeper into the sub components and processes of knowledge management that leaders need to get a handle on, namely, supplier-focused and customer-focused knowledge leadership.

Current wisdom on knowledge management draws from both resource-based and knowledge-based theories of the firm and documents the importance of the management of information and knowledge to the effective performance of organizations and also identifies a number of conditions under which knowledge management can be successful in terms of its organizational impact. The knowledge-based theory of the firm suggests that organizations can achieve a competitive advantage by the processes of creating knowledge and through the processes of integrating organizational knowledge through coordination mechanisms. Specifically, the knowledge-based theory of the firm explicitly focuses on the coordination mechanisms through which firms integrate the specialist knowledge of their members through appropriate organizational designs. Experts have identified different types of knowledge, such as tacit and explicit, episodic and procedural, know-how and know-why, in addition to different strategies for managing knowledge such as technological strategies and social (socio-cognitive) strategies.

Recently experts have also begun focusing more specifically on knowledge management across organizational boundaries. Two key constituents outside organizational boundaries that leaders and their organizations focus on are suppliers and customers. Such management of knowledge across organizational boundaries (vis-à-vis suppliers and customers) is a critical component or base of competitive advantage in today's global, technologically advanced environment. The difficulty in managing this knowledge resource has made it a critical leadership role.

WHAT IS CUSTOMER-FOCUSED KNOWLEDGE MANAGEMENT?

In addition to the social and technological components of Knowledge Management within the organizations described earlier, for the purpose of coordination, Knowledge Management experts also indicate that organizations manage the process through which they acquire and organize knowledge from outside the organization (e.g., from customers), and disseminate such knowledge and information within the organization. Processes that are set up for the specific enhancement of the data and information obtained from various entities in the environment such as customers (and/or suppliers) constitute a key component of Knowledge Management. Such processes can be labeled Customer-Focused Knowledge Management. Customer-focused knowledge management can manifest itself in practices like locating employees on the shop floor of customer organizations, key executives spending a significant amount of time with their customers, obtaining information from customers through electronic networks and information systems, and through the use of Knowledge Management systems within organizations that are focused especially on customers, such as customer meets and conferences. All of these practices and other similar ones can serve as vital sources of accurate information and knowledge that is of use to the focal organization, and can be termed customer-focused knowledge management. This concept is similar to what marketers call market orientation. Market orientation on the part of organizational executives has a significant positive impact on business performance.

WHAT IS SUPPLIER-FOCUSED KNOWLEDGE MANAGEMENT?

In addition to Knowledge Management processes focused on customers, such processes can also be focused on entities such as suppliers. Processes that are set up for the specific enhancement of the data and information obtained from suppliers constitute a key component of Knowledge Management. Such processes, focused on suppliers, can be labeled Supplier-Focused Knowledge Management. Supplier-focused knowledge management can manifest itself in practices like locating employees on the shop floor of supplier organizations, obtaining information from suppliers through electronic networks and information systems, and through the use of Knowledge Management systems within organizations that are focused especially on suppliers, among others such as practices targeted at enhancing supplier knowledge and involvement in the production process, and codesign of the components and modules provided by suppliers. All of these practices and other similar ones can serve as vital sources of accurate information and knowledge that is of use to the focal organization, and can be termed supplier-focused knowledge management.

MICHAEL DELL'S LEADERSHIP

As suggested earlier, the role of executive leaders in supplier-focused and customer-focused knowledge management and their positive impact on organizational performance is not well known. The study discussed here is based on the archival sources of information on Dell and its success in the computer industry and the specific examination of the interviews of Michael Dell in the business press. The data suggests that Michael Dell has invested a lot of time and effort in managing information and knowledge in the Dell Computer Corporation (now renamed Dell Inc.) since its establishment by him in the 1980s. In his interview with the editor of *Harvard Business Review* (Magretta 1998), Dell discusses the direct selling model that was pioneered by his firm in the computer industry and different facets of the company and the technology that made the direct sales model not only feasible, but also the root for a sustainable competitive advantage in that industry. A strong sense of customer-focus pervades Dell's responses in that interview. A major underlying factor in Dell's success is his focus on information and its management and its implications for managing the business at Dell Computers. In terms of information management, what the company does can be subdivided into a number of categories. At a broad level, one can distinguish between information that is internally available to the company versus that which is available from external sources such as customers and suppliers.

Dell's Customer-Focused Knowledge Management

Of the external sources of information, one can further subdivide it into information from the industry, in general, and the information provided by the customers, suppliers, etc. One of the key pieces of information (industry information) that drove the direct selling model of Dell computers is the fact that companies in the industry were focusing exclusively on vertical integration and on making all the key components within their premises. Thus, the extant business model was one of backward vertical integration. This information and its interpretation by Dell led the company to pick other suppliers for key components rather than making it on their own.

To add value to the process, Dell decided to eliminate the distributors (that is, it engaged in forward vertical integration as opposed to backward vertical integration) and sell his products directly to the customers to enhance both knowledge about customers and the relationship with them. In another interview, Dell said, "Well, we started the company by building to the customer's order. And interestingly enough, we didn't do it because we saw some massive paradigm in the future. Basically, we just didn't have any capital [to mass-produce]" (Murphy 1999). Luckily enough, this not only enhanced Dell's ability to know and understand customers better, but it also helped in making the process of delivering to the customer exactly what they wanted, much faster than other competitors. This also facilitates knowledge management by using better information management. This business model of direct selling was thus based on external information analysis to begin with. The analysis of external information available from customers is an ongoing process at Dell and this is made possible through the use of the Platinum Council meetings, the presence of their customer-service teams at the customer's site, and constant reception of information from the customers through these various channels and others such as the internet. Dell sums it up very nicely when he says the following:

> We turn our inventory over 30 times per year. If you look at the complexity and the diversity of our product line, there's no way we could do that unless we had credible information about what the customer is actually buying. It's a key part of why rivals have had great difficulty competing with Dell. It's not just that we sell direct, it's also our ability to forecast demand—it's both the design of the product and the way the information from the customer flows all the way through manufacturing to our suppliers. (Magretta 1998)

Interestingly enough, the comparative rate of inventory turnover at competitors is approximately 4.5. This difference alone contributes to a significant competitive edge for Dell vis-à-vis its competitors.

Dell keeps track of its customers over a period of time and analyzes their purchasing patterns to help in segmenting their customers. They call this process Fast-Cycle Segmentation, which is nothing but creating finer and finer segments of customers over a period of time as opposed to creating all the segments at one point in time and then trying to serve them all. This style of segmentation, in combination to what some call as sheer *profitability management*, is attributed to the huge growth in revenue that the company has obtained over a period of three years. Profitability management is about selecting the right customer groups to sell to, corporate customers being the most profitable group based on such analysis. Dell says, "People are sometimes surprised to learn that 90% of our sales go to institutions—business or government—and 70% to very large customers that buy at least $1 million PCs per year." Dell's impressive line of corporate customers includes Amazon.com, Bayerische Motoren Werke (BMW), British Airways, and Phillips, many of which have collaborative strategic alliances with Dell.

The underlying idea in this method of segmentation is that when information about a particular group of customers becomes significantly meaningful and distinct from those of other groups of customers, that is, when the information can be managed in a significantly better way by treating it as a separate segment and assigning a specific group of people to take care of that segment. Thus, their segmentation is also based on information and the load it puts on analysis and interpretation on the part of managers at Dell. Another key aspect of Dell's information management is their sales forecasting approach, which relies on qualitative information at the level of each customer rather than the aggregate and quantitative approach based on historic data that is popular with most companies. By focusing on information from each individual customer and their requirements, Dell is able to produce better forecasts and more real-time forecasts in a more accurate and precise fashion. From the point of view of information management, providing or sharing information with customers is as essential as getting information from them. Their interactive web sites and telephone lines that provide customers with all the available choices and potential troubleshooting answers help to achieve this.

Dell's Supplier-Focused Knowledge Management

"When we launch a new product, our suppliers' engineers are right in our plants. If a customer has a problem, we can fix it in real time" (Magretta 1998). With respect to suppliers, Dell provides more information (that is, information sharing) to them rather than receiving information from them. Suppliers of components are contracted for long terms and they are used as partners in facilitating the quick flow of products to Dell's customers, while at the same time ensuring that minimal inventory is maintained in the warehouses of both parties. Another key aspect (piece of information) of the competitive environment of the computer industry, that of obsolescence, drives this long term partnering with suppliers of key components and the necessity for maintaining low levels of inventory. In addition to facilitating low levels of inventory by smarter routing of components, the presence of suppliers' engineers on the shop floor of Dell's plants also helps in faster design and faster time to market for Dell's new products. This also facilitates faster problem solving for customers.

With respect to logistic suppliers such as Airborne Express or United Parcel Service (UPS), again Dell provides accurate information regarding the number of computers to be picked up from one of their plants and the corresponding number of monitors to be picked up from their supplier's plants and expects the logistics supplier to match this up and deliver to the customers based on the information provided. All this works because of excellent information management, in terms of sophisticated data exchange. Moreover, this is largely facilitated because of the direct selling model and the idea of building products based on customer orders and specifications. In Dell's own words:

> The technology available today really boosts the value of information sharing. We can share design databases and methodologies with supplier-partners in ways that just weren't possible five to ten years ago. This speeds time to market—often dramatically—and creates a lot of value that can be shared between buyer and supplier. (Magretta 1998)

Dell has slashed inventory turnover to an astonishing seven days, compared with 80 days or more for much of his competition. (In the computer industry, inventory loses 1 percent of its value for every week that it sits on the shelf; Dell's world-beating inventory management is thus critical to the company's bottom line.) Such world-beating inventory management is an outcome of the underlying supplier-focused knowledge management that misses the attention of most people. Dell has Kevin Rollins (Dell's co-CEO) to thank for all this excellent value-chain management and the shared leadership model the two have built, successfully so, in running the constantly changing firm's position in the tough computer industry with rivals constantly taking aim.

Dell's combination of effective customer-focused knowledge management and supplier-focused knowledge management helps them manage their value-chain in such an effective way that it achieves one of the greatest benefits of mass customization— unmatched levels of customer support, as evident by its lead in cor- porate customer satisfaction ratings over its competitors (*Business Wire* 2000, *PC World Online* 1999). The successful execution of such knowledge management has resulted in Dell being ranked No. 78 among the Fortune 500 companies and No. 210 in the Fortune Global 500. Dell Computer Corporation is the world's leading direct computer systems company, based on revenues of US$19.9 billion for the past four quarters (Edge: Work–Group Computing Report). Dell and Rollins lead the way and instituted many of the knowledge management and learning processes that are helping the company achieve record profits in the computer industry and in the other industries it perseveres to enter, such as consumer electronics. Dell says:

> When you have a company this large and this complex, it's truly important to have a very strong team. Kevin and I share the responsibilities of leading the company, developing the strategy and the execution. He does the hard stuff. I do the easy stuff. We share everything. He's been associated with the company in one form or another for many years, since arriving as a consultant in 1992. If you think about essentially every major decision that's been made for the past 10 years, Kevin has been right at the center of it. He's obviously key to the leadership of the company. (Exclusive interview in *The Chief Executive* 2003)

The role of executive leaders in Knowledge Management and its subcomponents such as customer-focused knowledge management and supplier-focused knowledge management are less recognized today in comparison to the credit they deserve. This chapter has dealt with all three of these components in the unique shared leadership success scenario of Dell Inc. in which Dell and Rollins manage information and knowledge vis-à-vis both customers and suppliers and seamlessly integrate Dell's make-to-order direct selling model. In addition, these leaders institute a rigorous program of training and development for their 20,000 plus employees to enable them to develop the right knowledge at the right time at which it is required. The examination of the archival sources and especially the interviews suggests that Knowledge Management in general, and both dimensions of supplier and customer-focused knowledge management play an integral role in the leadership of the firm once established by University of Texas student Dell in his garage in the 1980s. It is now the second largest computer manufacturer in the world and has a dominating presence in that market. Marketers have long realized the importance of market orientation and its effectiveness in contributing to performance. Customer-focused knowledge management starts with the basic concept of market orientation and builds on it by surrounding it with an organizational framework. Supply chain management has been vastly investigated in the computer, auto, and other manufacturing industries. None of these investigations realize the value of supplier-focused knowledge management and its impact on organizational performance. Using evidence from qualitative, archival, and interview data, this chapter has established that supplier-focused knowledge management, in addition to customer-focused knowledge management, has a positive impact on organizational performance and competitive advantage. More importantly, executive knowledge leadership is a critical component in making these types of activities instrumental to the organization. The significant amounts of investment made by Dell and the partnerships they have with universities to aid in the facilitation of learning and knowledge management is a key component of the organization's success.

6

SUPPLIER-FOCUSED KNOWLEDGE MANAGEMENT

BRAZIL'S AUTO INDUSTRY[1]

Suppliers can visit any Toyota facility with the possible exception of the new model design room. We hide nothing. But, they must be ready to open their plants to other network members.

—Koichiro Noguchi, Head of International Purchasing
(Dyer and Nobeoka 2000)

They gave us a gift [Toyota Production System, TPS]: how can we not open our plant and share what we've learned with other Toyota Suppliers.

—Executive at Summit Polymers (supplier to Toyota)
(Dyer and Nobeoka 2000)

V ery few companies engage in knowledge leadership across the value-chain to establish a strong competitive edge and an unbreakable hold on the marketplaces they operate in. Where Dell excels in both customer-focused and supplier-focused knowledge management, other companies in the automobile industry are well known for their learning reputation within their supplier network, namely, Toyota. Information and hence knowledge in these value-chains has become a key corporate resource and the necessity to manage that resource has become crucial with information explosion as a result of rapid growth in advanced information technologies, especially in emerging economies such as Brazil. Automobile companies in Brazil have extended concepts of supplier-focused knowledge management picked up from Japanese firms and employ both social networks and technological networks in managing such knowledge. Knowledge Management experts have documented the importance of the management of information and knowledge to the effective performance of organizations and have also identified a number of conditions under which knowledge management can be successful in terms of its organizational impact. These experts argue that organizations can achieve a competitive advantage by the processes of creating knowledge and through the processes of integrating organizational knowledge through co-ordination mechanisms.

The tendency to view customers and suppliers, or other entities, outside of what are traditional organizational boundaries, as potential sources of organizational knowledge, in addition to being potential recipients, is fairly new. Viewing these entities as part of the broader network and thus being considered as 'us' rather than as 'them' is the reason for including them in knowledge sharing networks. Given that such thinking is fairly new, there is relatively little discussion among experts on the impact of subcomponents and processes of Knowledge Management on organizational performance. Our focus in this chapter on supplier-focused knowledge management is fairly new and has not appeared in the relevant literatures. Experts in supplier-relations, the closest set of professionals, have focused mainly on ideas, such as transaction costs, asset and location specificity, and collaborative versus adversarial relations, with the focus on concepts such as modularization, a topic related to knowledge management, and knowledge sharing, being relatively new. Supplier-focused knowledge management, as briefly defined in the previous chapter, can be seen as knowledge management within supplier-relations. Manufacturers in the Brazilian auto industry have successfully replicated and extended supplier-focused knowledge management concepts to achieve higher levels of product and business performance.

An examination of practices within the Brazilian auto industry and Toyota's knowledge sharing network suggests that knowledge leadership in and among the network of suppliers is very crucial for overall organizational performance in the long run and takes the following forms. In other words, executives desiring to exhibit knowledge leadership in the supply side of their value-chains need to pay attention to the following:

1. Executives with the desire to exhibit knowledge leadership in the supply side of the value-chain should first start by implementing knowledge sharing initiatives vis-à-vis suppliers. These knowledge-sharing initiatives should span both face-to-face knowledge sharing via socio-cognitive networks, and electronic knowledge sharing via technological networks. Both of these are important, and one is not a substitute for the other.

2. Executives, in the attempt to implement knowledge leadership, should take care to institute an inducement-contribution system to motivate the participants in the manufacturer-supplier chain or the broader supplier network. The broad objective of the inducement-contribution system is to motivate people to contribute to the system by actively sharing knowledge, in addition to the objective of avoiding free riders by having appropriate penalty mechanisms.

3. In addition to direct knowledge sharing, executives wanting to exhibit knowledge leadership should also integrate the suppliers' activities with their production process. Supplier teams or mini supplier units can be located at the manufacturer's premises to enhance and facilitate such supplier integration into the production process. Alternatively, the process of workflow from the supplier plant to the manufacturer's plant can be analyzed and the same can/should be reengineered to make it more efficient by removing duplications and redundancies. The chain of processes should be made more effective by a better understanding of the interdependencies involved in the whole transition process. This step is likely to take some time for the participants to adjust to the coordination needs and interdependency optimization.

4. Executives intending to provide knowledge leadership should also institute the practice of early supplier involvement in product design by throwing open their factories to trustworthy suppliers and requiring them to dovetail their design function with that of the manufacturer. These suppliers should be asked to develop designs for their products that are in tune with the changing demands of the marketplace, in addition to constantly improving designs, which would otherwise not be possible in the absence of knowledge of manufacturing processes.

5. Knowledge leadership will demand first and foremost that these executives deal with the people issues involved in this entire process outlined in the aforementioned steps. Building trust, building a climate of knowledge sharing, and other issues described in the chapter on micro knowledge leadership are doubly important within the context of the steps in the supplier network discussed earlier. In addition to the people issues, knowledge leaders will also do well to focus on the technological issues surrounding these processes and facilitate them as well.

This chapter provides a model of supplier-focused knowledge management and its impact on product and financial performance. The chapter is based on evidence on the sharing and management of knowledge resources across organizational boundaries as an explicit component of collaborative relations (for example, vis-à-vis suppliers), in the context of Brazil's auto industry. This evidence is combined with knowledge of Toyota's production system and their highly effective knowledge-sharing network of suppliers. The focus on Brazil serves to throw some light on some non-Japanese companies that have taken advantage of such supplier-focused knowledge sharing and made it to work in an emerging economy with huge physical infrastructure problems, not unlike those in other emerging markets of the world. This chapter uses advances in the Knowledge Management and supplier-relations fields of knowledge to develop the broad model of supplier-focused knowledge management.

This chapter delineates the processes through which knowledge management vis-à-vis suppliers affects financial and product performance in the Brazilian automotive industry. Knowledge Management experts draw on the organizational learning, organizational memory and related fields of knowledge and extend the core concepts by discussing the location of knowledge vis-à-vis information in a semiotic framework. In this framework, stimulus, data, information, and knowledge lie on successively higher levels of abstraction, possibly with wisdom occupying the highest level. Knowledge has been referred to in terms of a set of beliefs about causal relationships between actions and their probable consequences. Knowledge has also been defined as information that has been processed and interpreted in a certain context within which it is embedded. Some experts define Knowledge Management as an organizational capability that allows people in organizations, working as individuals, or in teams, projects, or other such communities of interest to create, capture, share, and leverage their collective knowledge to improve competitiveness and performance. Other experts conceptualize the concept of Knowledge Management as the concern for creation of such structures that combine the most advanced elements of technological resources and the indispensable input of human response and decision-making. Putting processes in place, containing a massive amount of information, organizing it logically, and making it accessible to the right people are all key components of such a view of Knowledge Management. Internal benchmarking efforts to share knowledge-creating strategic alliances, investments in training and development, and the building of computer based information repositories and systems, have all been seen as key components of Knowledge Management.

As described earlier, two broad approaches have been identified to the management of knowledge in organizations—the personalization approach and the codification approach. The personalization approach includes face-to-face communication, communication through such structures as networks of people, cross-functional teams, committees, task forces, training and development, internal knowledge sharing through benchmarking and job rotation, and creation of strategic alliances. The codification approach refers to the technological route for knowledge management and includes the setting up of databases, data warehouses, decision support systems, Enterprise Resource Planning (ERP) systems, and electronic networks for communication and sharing knowledge.

SUPPLIER-FOCUSED KNOWLEDGE MANAGEMENT

In addition to the social and technological components of Knowledge Management within organizations described earlier, for the purpose of coordination, organizations manage the process through which they acquire, and organize knowledge from outside the organization (for example, from suppliers), and disseminate such knowledge and information within the organization. The processes that are set up for the specific enhancement of the data and information obtained from various entities in the environment, such as suppliers, constitute a key component of Knowledge Management. Such processes, focused on suppliers, can be labeled supplier-focused knowledge management.

Although information on supplier-relations in the auto industry has been developing for some time, the specific focus on collaboration with suppliers for knowledge sharing purposes is fairly new. Most of the experts in this field have focused on supplier-relations using ideas, such as transaction costs, collaborative versus adversarial relations, and variables such as asset specificity and location specificity. A focus on collaborative supplier-relationships for knowledge sharing purposes is a very important determinant of competitive advantage in the automobile industry, among others such as pharmaceuticals, and hence the need to examine such knowledge management vis-à-vis suppliers has gained increased importance. Several processes are involved in the management of knowledge vis-à-vis suppliers in the Brazilian automobile industry. These processes are described in the supplier-focused knowledge management model and their impact on product and financial performance is identified.

A Model of Supplier-Focused Knowledge Management

This model is provided for use by executives intending to demonstrate knowledge leadership vis-à-vis suppliers in their organizations. The model draws from and builds on the knowledge bases in the fields of Knowledge Management and Supplier-Relations. The four broad dimensions of supplier-focused knowledge management are (a) supplier knowledge sharing; (b) supplier knowledge integration to the production process; (c) early supplier involvement in product design through the use of Knowledge Management tools; and (d) instituting an inducement-contribution system for facilitating all of the three previous dimensions. These dimensions are blended into the model of the relationship between supplier-focused knowledge management and performance, in the context of the industry and its customers, as can be seen in Figure 6.1. The model in Figure 6.1 suggests that supplier-focused knowledge management has a direct and positive impact on financial and product performance.

The essence of the supplier-focused knowledge management model shown here is that it has a favorable impact on product performance as identified by its various characteristics, such as cost, speed to market, quality, and reputation, in addition to its independent effect on financial performance. The model shows three components that enhance collaboration between suppliers and manufacturers with the focus on sharing and managing knowledge. The fourth dimension of supplier-focused knowledge management ensures that the other three dimensions are in working order and contribute positively to the organization. In other words this fourth dimension ensures the overall climate is in place for the core activities of supplier-focused knowledge management to proceed uninhibited.

Supplier knowledge sharing

Recent experiences in supplier-relations within the auto industry have identified the importance of knowledge sharing and the building of a network for such purposes. However, indications to the effect that collaborative supplier-relations and information sharing in a network mode are likely determinants of competitive advantage in this industry have been around for a long time. Some experts have evidence that suggests that specialized networks of suppliers provide a competitive advantage to manufacturers in the auto industry. In one such study, one aspect of specificity—location specificity— was closely thought to be linked to the degree of information sharing between supplier and manufacturer. The degree of such information sharing is a crucial component of supplier-focused knowledge management. Locating suppliers within a manufacturer's premises does not automatically guarantee a high degree of information sharing and thus it is an independent task remaining to be executed.

Figure 6.1
SUPPLIER-FOCUSED KNOWLEDGE MANAGEMENT

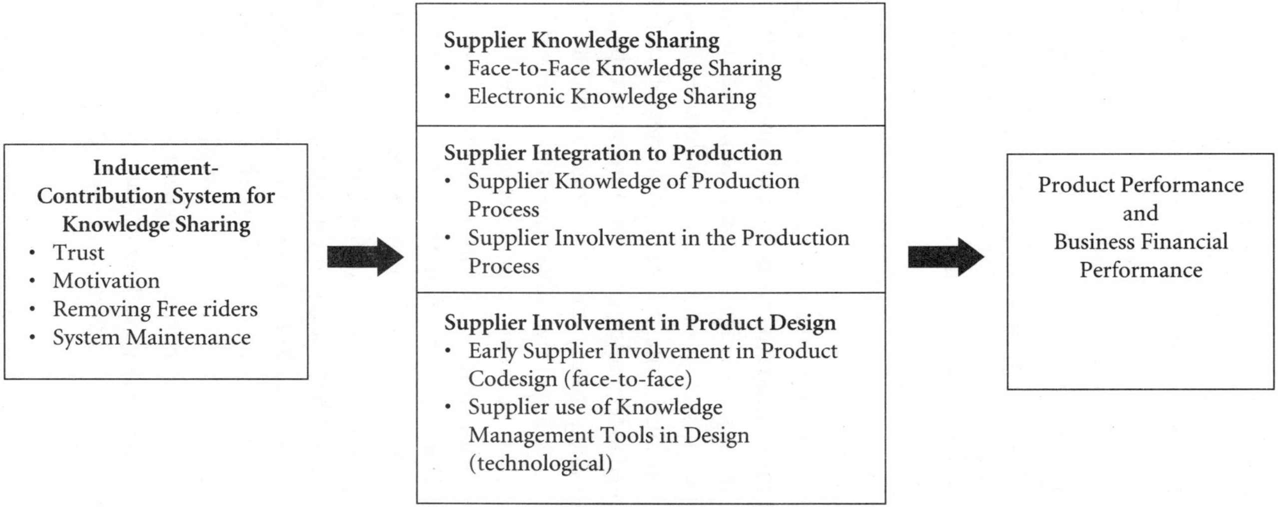

**Inducement-
Contribution System for
Knowledge Sharing**
- Trust
- Motivation
- Removing Free riders
- System Maintenance

Supplier Knowledge Sharing
- Face-to-Face Knowledge Sharing
- Electronic Knowledge Sharing

Supplier Integration to Production
- Supplier Knowledge of Production Process
- Supplier Involvement in the Production Process

Supplier Involvement in Product Design
- Early Supplier Involvement in Product Codesign (face-to-face)
- Supplier use of Knowledge Management Tools in Design (technological)

Product Performance
and
Business Financial
Performance

However, such collocation does facilitate smoother and faster flow of information and knowledge in the supplier-manufacture chain in both directions. The presence of a strong electronic and telecommunications infrastructure provides an alternative in instances where collocation is not possible, because knowledge sharing can also happen without location specificity. However, both the social network advantage of collocation and the technological network advantage are necessary for effective knowledge sharing. In that sense they are not mutually exclusive elements of supplier-focused knowledge management.

In addition to information sharing, some experts also emphasize the resulting benefit of conversion of tacit knowledge to explicit knowledge through these supplier networks as an important element contributing to competitive advantage in the auto industry. The nature of knowledge sharing practices at Toyota within their own network and sub-networks is reflective of such knowledge conversion. Such interpersonal processes of knowledge sharing (as opposed to technological routes) are more capable of converting tacit knowledge to explicit knowledge, a crucial component contributing to competitive advantage. This is why it is important to reiterate that the technological networks for knowledge sharing are not meant to be a substitute for the face-to-face knowledge sharing. Knowledge sharing through both media rich, face-to-face communication and through technological networks such as electronic data transfer and reliance on Knowledge Management tools are imperative in the knowledge sharing component of supplier-focused knowledge management. Manufacturers that engage in higher levels of knowledge sharing with suppliers through face-to-face communication enjoy higher levels of performance. Manufacturers that engage in higher levels of knowledge sharing with suppliers through technological knowledge management and electronic information transfer enjoy higher levels of performance.

Supplier integration in the production process

Although supplier-relations experts have mainly focused on the innovation benefits of close ties with suppliers in the product development process, such close relations with suppliers and integration into the production process also provides several benefits in the manufacturing realm. Suppliers possessing knowledge of the manufacturer's production process and integration into their production provides benefits, such as reduced costs in multiple areas, flexibility under varying demand conditions, reduced risk of disrupted deliveries, possibility of sequencing production of pre-assemblies and assemblies, and the potential for experiential learning by producing a focused set of components/products over the long run. Such benefits occurred in the context of 'Local Assembly Units (LAUs)' near manufacturers. However, such local units achieved these benefits only by engaging in higher levels of interactions (both face-to-face and through Electronic Data Interchanges) resulting in higher knowledge of the production process and higher integration into the production process of the manufacturer. A study conducted by the author[2] provides quantitative evidence of such supplier knowledge of the production process, integration into the production process, and the resulting impact of these on product and financial performance.

Increased knowledge of the interdependencies of the production process and of the interfaces in such processes spans across both manufacturing and product development processes, since these are fundamentally interlinked. Evidence is available from the pharmaceutical industry for the positive link between knowledge and the product development process, especially in terms of the time for development. Within the context of the supplier-focused knowledge management model, increased levels of supplier knowledge of the production process leads to more collaborative efforts with manufacturers. As suggested earlier, higher levels of supplier knowledge integration into the production process makes these supplier-manufacturer chains more highly capable of structuring and organizing the production process to provide more flexibility and quickness and the competitiveness resulting from it. Higher levels of supplier involvement in the production process is also necessary to prepare them for higher levels of sharing knowledge and thus easier conversion of tacit knowledge about interfaces and interdependencies to explicit knowledge. Such conversion is crucial for firms trying to build specialized networks with suppliers to build their competitive advantage.

Information technologies and flexible manufacturing technologies have allowed for the inexpensive modification of production set ups and sequences and thereby increase the inter-firm know-how of their specific interfaces. Although these technologies increase the resource availabilities in these areas, the actual competitive advantages accrue only to those firms that have the capabilities to utilize these technology and knowledge resources, as evidenced by the motivational challenges, among others, faced by Toyota in building its supplier network to share knowledge, and the difficulties faced by North American firms to replicate such links. Thus, it becomes imperative to enhance actual levels of supplier knowledge of the production process and their level of integration into the manufacturer's production process, because these are the crucial underlying variables that impact product and financial performance. In Brazil, mainly non-Japanese automakers have taken painstaking efforts at improving suppliers' knowledge of the manufacturers' production process and in integrating such knowledge with the focal production units. Among Brazilian automakers and their suppliers, higher levels of supplier knowledge of the production process are positively related to higher levels of performance. In addition, higher levels of supplier involvement in the production process are positively related to higher levels of performance.

Supplier early involvement in product design

In addition to supplier involvement in the production process, involvement in the earlier stages, namely, design, can improve crucial capabilities such as anticipating for and designing for tacit knowledge of interdependencies and for managing interdependencies in an optimal manner to enhance ongoing quickness of the process and its flexibility. Some experts have touched on the innovation benefits of close ties with suppliers in the product development process. It has become common practice in the auto industry for suppliers to set up shop within the manufacturer's premises and to be involved in the project right from the design phase. Such practices maximize location specificity, which are strongly connected to information and knowledge sharing. Such knowledge sharing is in the specific form of technical exchange and cooperation in the technological realm. Thus, early involvement of the suppliers in the product development and manufacturing process, in the form of collaborative design and in the form of technical exchange and cooperation, is a critical component of the supplier-focused knowledge management. Such early supplier involvement in design has a significant impact on performance in the auto industry in terms of both product and financial performance.

Information systems for knowledge management and technological knowledge management tools contribute significantly to organization performance. Specific Knowledge Management systems, built on custom-designed knowledge management architectures have been utilized by Brazilian automakers to contribute strongly to organizational performance. The codification approach to knowledge management is entirely consistent with this view of the impact of the technological route to knowledge management. The supplier's early involvement in product design in the form of higher levels of interaction between suppliers and manufacturers using technological knowledge management tools, as well as the early involvement of suppliers through codesign, results in higher levels of product and financial performance.

Conditions for effectiveness of supplier-focused knowledge management

Increasing levels of knowledge sharing in manufacturer-supplier combinations have an important impact on competitive advantage of organizations by providing the capability to handle environmental change more effectively. Higher levels of collaborative relationships focused on knowledge sharing provides firms with the capabilities to reduce costs, bring products to market quicker, stabilize and improve quality, and reduce risk of disruptions, all of which cushion the effect of environmental change. It is important for executives to realize that such supplier-focused knowledge management can become more critical under conditions of rapid environmental change. Such rapid environmental change may demand higher levels of knowledge sharing, creation, and leveraging vis-à-vis suppliers. Specifically, rapid technological changes in the design and manufacture of assemblies, sub-assemblies, and focal production units make supplier-focused knowledge management more important and therefore more strongly associated with performance, than under other conditions. There is some evidence to suggest that there is generally a greater willingness to share knowledge in emerging economy enterprises than those in developed economies. Brazil's auto parts industry has been identified as a 'hot' sector with high growth rates. This, in combination with the presence of highly competitive steel, glass, and rubber industries, and massive investments to the technology sector of Brazil makes for a highly dynamic economic and technological environment. It is no wonder then that Brazilian automakers have engaged in higher levels of supplier-focused knowledge management and found success in such a context.

When competitors introduce new products using new technologies at a rapid pace, thereby increasing the level of product variety, it forces all manufacturers to respond strategically or put themselves in the strategic position of being able to respond to such changes. Knowledge Management in general and supplier-focused knowledge management in particular serves to provide this capability of flexibility and quick response. Additionally, under conditions of rapid technological change, the conversion of tacit knowledge to explicit knowledge becomes more challenging and calls for increased levels of interaction, collaboration, cooperation, and knowledge sharing. This is because the bases of both tacit and explicit knowledge change with the rapid changes in the technology. Thus, rapid changes in product design and the manufacturing process, as is the case in the auto industry, necessitates higher levels of knowledge management between suppliers and manufacturers, without which the manufacturer's strategic flexibility and responsive ability is likely to suffer. This is similar to what has been experienced in the global computer manufacturing industry. When there was a high-level of uncertainty, in the form of unpredictable products, which is relatively constant and high, higher levels of supplier involvement in the production process were required to improve product performance in the form of speed of product development. Thus, such kind of knowledge management becomes more important under conditions of high technological change than under conditions of low technological change. This is true for each of the four dimensions of supplier-focused knowledge management identified earlier. High-levels of (a) face-to-face knowledge sharing; (b) electronic knowledge exchange; (c) supplier knowledge of the production process; (d) supplier involvement in the production process; (e) supplier early involvement in product codesign; and (f) use of technological knowledge management tools in design are all important when there is rapid technological change in the manufacturing context. Under such conditions, it is important for all of the above to be facilitated with a fairly effective system of inducements-contributions to motivate and facilitate the knowledge management process. There is higher demand on this overarching system of inducements-contributions, especially under conditions of rapidly changing technology.

NOTES

1. I gratefully acknowledge the conceptual contributions from Ronaldo Parente who co-authored a study on Brazilian automakers.
2. The study was done in collaboration with Ronaldo Parente.

7

MANAGING CHANGE THROUGH KNOWLEDGE LEADERSHIP

JACK WELCH AT GE

Managers traditionally haven't shared information Information was power, so they held it back. They saw their job as control. I see that as unproductive, a waste of energy.

—**Welch on GE managers and their attitudes vis-à-vis boundarylessness**
(Lakshman 2007a)

I nformation and hence knowledge has become a key corporate resource, and the necessity to manage it has become crucial with information explosion as a result of technologies such as the internet. Management Information Systems (MIS) experts on knowledge management highlight its importance to ensure effective performance of organizations (Armstrong and Sambamurthy 1999: 304–27; Davenport et al. 1998; and Zack 1999: 45–58). Leadership experts identify attributes, such as business knowledge, behaviors such as information search, acquisition, and use, and contingencies such as knowledge and information requirements of decision situations (Day and Lord 1988: 453–64; and Fleishman et al. 1991: 245–87). This chapter brings together all of these knowledge sources with a case study of one of the most hailed top executives of corporate America (namely, Jack Welch) to identify and explicate the role of executives in knowledge management and their knowledge-based change strategies in organizations. Although a countless number of articles, interviews, and published works (including a few cases) exist on his leadership style, none focus on his knowledge leadership. The study reveals that effective executives play an active role in knowledge leadership through mechanisms such as destroying the Not Invented Here (NIH) syndrome, instituting programs of internal and external knowledge transfer, establishing communities of learning, knowledge-based human resource strategies, and Information Technology (IT) based knowledge management systems, among others. This chapter details some of these Knowledge Leadership approaches and their impact on performance.

Most business professionals, academicians, consultants, and practitioners alike, have hailed Jack Welch as one of the best CEOs of the century. General Electric (GE) has been the most admired corporation for five years in a row, thanks to the legendary role played by its tough and determined former CEO Welch, who stepped down in September 2001. Welch had been named the most admired CEO for a few years, thanks to the performance of the company under his watch (*GE Annual Report* 2001). Regardless of the post-retirement controversies about lavish perks and excessive retirement income, brought to the forefront by the recent troubles he has undergone on the domestic front through divorce proceedings undertaken by his wife, many academics and practitioners still opine that his legacy will live on for years to come and that Welch will continue to be a role model for future CEOs.

The famous GE management development institute at Crotonville, usually referred to as the Croton-on-Hudson, has recently been renamed as the John F. Welch Learning Center in honor of this CEO who made such effective use of the learning center in transferring knowledge and sharing organizational values, and made it a key component of GE's effectiveness over the last 20 years (*GE Annual Report* 2001). The 3098 percent growth in GE's stock since April 1, 1981, when Welch took over as CEO of GE, an annual average growth rate of 18.9 percent (comparable figures for the S&P are 896 percent and 12.2 percent, respectively), gives an indication of the nature of the accomplishment Welch's GE has achieved (Serwer 2001: 237–38).

The magnificent scale of his achievement silences and muffles voices of the critics and their assertions of Welch being over-lionized, over-valued, and their allegations of impropriety in the social responsibility realm, such as the downsizing issue and the issue of the PCBs in the Hudson River. Despite criticisms and questions about over-romanticization of leadership in general or leadership of Welch in particular, Welch remains far above the rest of the CEOs of his time in terms of both the processes he established at the company, those that he refined, and the outcomes that speak volumes and belies the Herculean efforts that served and continue to serve as the foundation for the company's strength today and into the distant future.

BACKGROUND

GE is a diversified conglomerate operating in a dozen or so businesses in wide ranging fields, such as lighting, medical systems, transportation, plastics, industrial systems, financial services, aerospace, and aircraft engines. During the peak of his reign as GE's chairman, Welch undertook and implemented massive divestitures, downsizing, and acquisitions of a number of businesses, following his visionary principle of being No. 1 or No. 2 in all of the businesses that GE operates in, and thus competing from a position of strength. Those that did not meet the criterion of being No. 1 or No. 2 were either fixed so they obtained that position of strength, or closed because there was no reasonable way of obtaining that position, or sold to other operators because the business did not fit into the distinctive and core competencies of the corporation. Welch stated in the 1983 annual report, "You're either the best at what you do or you don't do it for very long." With earnings of US$14.1 billion on revenues of US$125.9 billion in 2001, GE presented a picture of a healthy conglomerate in a solid position for even further future growth in earnings. Investors holding GE stock for a period of five years including 2001 obtained an average 21 percent annual return on their investment, and those holding their stock for 10 years averaged a 23 percent total annual return. Clearly, the long-term performance is great and long-term prospects for the company are bright, by virtue of being in businesses that have "staying power",[1] in the words of Welch. In 1981, when Jack Welch took over as CEO, only lighting, motors, and power systems were leaders in their markets. By 1992, all of GE's businesses were either No. 1 or No. 2 in their respective markets.

WHY DID JACK WELCH WANT A REVOLUTION?

Although Welch did not inherit a company that was either weak or in poor financial condition, he wanted a revolution after taking upon the job of CEO. GE under his predecessor Reginald Jones was in very good financial position. Under Jones, revenue had grown at an average annual rate of 12 percent, with earnings growing at an annual rate of 16 percent. Reginald Jones had been named the most admired CEO of 1980 according to a Fortune survey when Welch took over office. GE was named the best-managed company at that same time (Colvin 1999). Clearly, Welch was handed a company that was in a position of strength, just as his successor Jeff Immelt was handed one of the most valuable companies in the world. So why did Jack Welch want a revolution? Why was he chosen over four other candidates by his predecessor Jones? According to Noel Tichy, Professor, University of Michigan, and long time observer (both inside and outside observer) of Jack Welch, he was chosen for both his strong performance record and for his future plans (including a revolution) for GE if he was made the CEO (Tichy and Sherman 1992).

Jack Welch felt that the financial strength of GE on paper hid a number of weaknesses that could surface to trouble GE in the near future. To outsiders it may have been a case of spotting trouble before it happened. However, to Welch, a man that demanded that his subordinates and scores of GE managers face reality as it were rather than how they wished it were, reality presented a different picture. He noted in several interviews that a number of GE businesses were not in very strong competitive positions at the end of 1980, although they were all making money from orders won in previous years. Jones, having had a finance background, had pooled together a few businesses, such as the coal mining business, through acquisitions, to simply smoothen revenue streams, rather than choosing these businesses for their strategic fit with the corporation.

Welch also was keenly aware of the impending globalization and the resulting heightened competitive nature of business after business that would further weaken the not so strong position of GE. Thus, a combination of external environmental changes, a few prior actions that were financial portfolio approaches rather than competency portfolio approaches, and weakening businesses depending on prior years' orders for earnings presented a picture of reality to Welch that was less than flattering. Thus, having a keen sense of perception of reality and having the vantage position of the insider, Jack Welch wanted nothing less than a revolution. A revolution is what Jack Welch brought about at GE. As suggested by leadership researchers, Jack Welch possessed very complete and accurate knowledge in the form of cause-effect beliefs.[2]

He had downsized GE significantly and laid off or displaced nearly a 100,000 of the corporation's 400,000 employees over the period of his first eight years in office. As early as 1984, three years into his CEO tenure, Welch had overseen the divestiture of some 117 businesses or pieces of business units from coal mines to light'n easy irons, representing a fifth of GE's asset base of US$21 billion. Combined with these downsizing initiatives and sale of businesses that were either under performing or lacked a fit with the core competencies, Welch engineered a number of acquisitions of businesses that served to strengthen existing businesses and moved them to a No. 1 or No. 2 competitive position. The acquisitions of Tungsram Lighting in Hungary and the purchase of a lighting business in Britain were of this nature. There were other acquisitions that strengthened the entire corporation and aimed at affirming the identity of the corporation.

STRUCTURING FOR INFORMATION AND KNOWLEDGE TRANSFER

The acquisition of Radio Corporation of America (RCA, once owned by GE and sold to investors), along with National Broadcasting Company (NBC), was a major acquisition that was made at a time when Jack Welch was taking a lot of heat from many corners and was even named Neutron Jack for the massive layoffs implemented by him. In addition, Welch subjected the organization's structure to restructuring, what he called delayering, to enhance communication and transfer of information between the businesses and the CEO's office, without any intervening layers filtering the information and transferring the information at a much more rapid pace in either direction, increasing the speed of business. Speed was one of the core business values of Jack Welch, along with simplicity and self-confidence.

Along with such internal structural changes, he also wanted an organization-wide sharing of information and knowledge in the form of ongoing, no-holds-barred debates on issues and problems being faced. This he implemented through the instruments of the Chief Executive Council (CEC) and the fabled *work-out* process. He also had teams of executives from across divisions working on problems at the learning center (Crotonville), and a number of teams that were leading the work-out process at each of the individual businesses. In all, he was getting the organization to exhibit his principled value of boundarylessness, which according to him was an open sharing of information of all kinds, without regard to any boundaries. All of these internal organizational initiatives served to share and disseminate knowledge in a way that rendered the whole organization more effective than before. The results of all these changes over a period of 20 years were more than adequate. Under Welch, GE moved from a market capitalization of US$13 billion to just over US$490 billion. Under Welch, GE's revenues had grown from around US$26.8 billion to nearly US$130 billion. GE averaged a solid 12 percent annual earnings growth throughout Welch's time at the top and about 15 percent over the last eight years (Walker 2001: 22–26).

THE EARLY YEARS

Having acquired a PhD in Chemical Engineering at the University of Illinois in 1960, Dr Jack Welch took a US$10,500 per year engineering position with GE in Pittsfield Massachusetts. There he felt so disappointed and stifled by the bureaucracy of the scientifically managed corporation, in addition to feeling under-appreciated, that he decided to take up another job offer despite a US$1,000 pay raise. One of the executives of the company, Reuben Gutoff, positioned a level above him in the organization, unhappy with Welch's decision and desperate to keep the talented young man that he was impressed with, coaxed Welch and his wife out to dinner. There Gutoff persuaded Welch for over four hours by promising to minimize or eliminate red tape and provide a small company environment for Jack Welch to operate in with autonomy, themes that would later dominate Welch's own attempt at leading the corporation (Byrne 1998). Indeed, the elimination of highly bureaucratic work processes and layers of organizational bureau-cracy, in addition to getting the company and its managers to share information regardless of hierarchy or boundary or official channels, were key components of Welch's information and know-ledge management approach to leading GE. Thereafter, Welch would stubbornly remain in Pittsfield, Massachusetts (MA), for 17 years, despite taking on higher level positions that normally required other executives to move to the Fairfield, Connecticut (CT), headquarters.

In 1968, Jack Welch took over as the General Manager (GM) for the plastics business, having been promoted over four management layers in the span of his 8 years at GE. His disdain for bureaucracy and passion for information sharing stayed with him throughout his career. He always had a tough nose for business. His decision-making methods had not changed much since his days in the plastics industry. He gathered everyone he could find who knew something about the subject at hand—whether chemists, production engineers, or finance people—and thoroughly debriefed them. He wanted on-the-spot answers, not formal, written reports. Then he would join his subordinates in fierce, no-holds-barred debates about which decision to make. Some observers characterized Jack Welch as an information junkie (Tichy and Sherman 1992). He had no patience for formal reports. He would just drop in on people and engage in conversations with them, grill them, and obtain the necessary information he needed for decisions.

This method of decision-making would later show up in his delayering of GE, the removal of the entire top layer of executives, who went between the CEO's office and the business leaders. He was frustrated with the process when either the executives that belonged to this layer were not able to answer the questions he had or they had to check back with the individual business leaders to obtain that information. Welch felt that trying to move information through layer after layer in an organization was like playing the children's game of telephone: the data get corrupted, the reality gets obscured, and that was an absolute no-no, as far as Welch was concerned. His predecessors had instituted massive studies by reputed consultants and the detailed analysis and reports in the form of blue books were available to the scores of GE managers. Welch simply scorned those blue books and figuratively burnt them. Welch wanted his managers and employees to think themselves, analyze situations, and make decisions on their own, without being tied down by the blue books, even though these books represented the ideas of some of the best American thinkers such as Peter Drucker. He wanted his business leaders (he preferred the word leaders over managers) to take charge of their businesses, get headquarters out of their hair, fight the bureaucracy, hate it, kick it, break it.

JACK AS AN INFORMATION JUNKIE

Nothing could get in his quest for information. He would scorn organizational charts and roam freely within the organization, cultivating his own sources of information among relatively low-ranking executives. This network of information sometimes provided him with such knowledge about a particular business or situation that even the people who ran those businesses were not as knowledgeable as Welch, on a given day. One of the things that executives would find out quick enough is that Welch had a penchant for discussion and debate and wanted his executives to be able to answer tough questions, which he felt were necessary to ensure that plans wouldn't go awry. This required self-confidence on the part of the managers, one of the core business values Welch wanted GE to have, in addition to speed and simplicity. In an interview for *Harvard Business Review*, Welch said, "For a large organization to be effective, it must be simple. For a large organization to be simple, its people must have self-confidence and intellectual assurance. Clear, tough-minded people are the most simple." Insecure managers create complexity. Frightened, nervous managers use thick convoluted planning books and busy slides filled with everything they've known since childhood. Real leaders don't need clutter. People must have the self-confidence to be clear, precise, to be sure that every person in their organization—highest to lowest—understands what the business is trying to achieve. But it's not easy. You can't believe how hard it is for people to be simple, how much they fear being simple. They worry that if they're simple, people will think that they're simpleminded. In reality of course, it's just the reverse. Clear, tough-minded people are the most simple.

In 1973 he was named group head for plastics and medical systems (General Electric Medical Systems [GEMS]). As the head of this group of businesses, he continued to display his tough-mindedness, acute sense of perception, and continued to use similar decision-making methods as at plastics. He would be in serious contention for the top organizational position in a few years, having demonstrated enough success to move up the organization this far. His keen sense of reality and nose for tough businesses made him succeed in tough situations. A few years before he became group head of both the plastics and medical systems units, he made some tough product choices in plastics, taking advantage of the creative work done by his Research and Development (R&D) people in the lab. They developed a new kind of polypropylene plastic material called NORYL. In the face of tough competition and information uncertainty about the potential success of this new product over the conventional polystyrene, Welch decided to go with the new product, one that GE continues on with to this day. Combined with this tough choice he had his sales people develop applications for this product rather than sell only to customers that already had applications for this product. This application development approach to new products generated by the laboratory helped them to achieve record orders from the automobile industry and thus kick-start the plastics unit's revenues and profitability. This was a decision that was made in the typical process of getting to-gether people with relevant information, going through a process of debating the pros and cons, facing reality as clearly as possible through tough questions, and finally making a decision that most people would own and commit to.

Through such decisions and more, as head of this new group of businesses, Welch embodied several values that he would display in future assignments as the head of the consumer products group and as CEO of the organization. He always emphasized the practice of planful opportunism, taking advantage of opportunities through careful planning. One of the other values he embodied was that of wallowing in information until you find the simple solution. In this process of being immersed in information, he believed in testing ideas through creative conflict, a concept that manifested itself in his approach to the discussions of the executive council at Crotonville (now the John F. Welch Learning Center), the organization-wide debates through the work-out process, and other periodic meetings with executives and employees. He tried to implement the value of treating all subordinates as equals, but rewarding each one according to merit. Treating subordinates as equals is well documented in Jack Welch's quest for informality in most settings. In most in-stances, the focus of his approach was cultivating information sources at low-ranking levels in the organization, not relying on formal reports or formal wear, getting into free-flowing discussions, and focusing on people, their problems, and ways to solve those problems. At the same time he believed in not compromising when making decisions. He never compromised on his disdain for bureaucracy and the resulting dismantling of the hierarchy and eventual replacement with close knit teams of people. Reportedly, he wanted to get underneath the skin of people to motivate them. He wanted to give people every chance to identify with their business and said that, "Their enthusiasm is your most valuable asset" (Collingwood and Coutu 2002). Answering a question on how to make a small company environment in the business, in an interview, Welch said:

> Get into the skin of every person so they know that their ideas count. Celebrate small successes. Evaluate the people down to the lowest units, so they know that their achievements are constantly being measured and that they count. It's critical that people know that their contributions matter. It's critical that they know what they do will be seen and rewarded. It's pretty simple really. Simplicity is the essence of managing people. (Collingwood and Coutu 2002)

WELCH AS CANDIDATE FOR CEO SUCCESSION

It was in 1977 that Jack Welch started really contending for the CEO's position when Jones and his Executive Management Staff (EMS) picked six candidates through a fairly detailed review process consisting of interviews, investigation of performance records, and the like. Each of the six candidates was then assigned to a business group that was new to him. Welch got assigned to the consumer products and services groups, moving him out of his Pittsfield, MA, base which he held for a long time despite being group head for both plastics and medical systems. It was in 1977 at the consumer products group that the explicit realization dawned on Welch (still much sooner than many of his peers) that information was more valuable and more powerful than any hard asset.

It happened at GE Capital. When I got involved with GE capital in 1977, I had been making things all my life, making products. Then, I was given the responsibility for GE capital, which was then still a very small business. We had all the capital in the world, and all we needed to make money was ideas. That was a revelation to me. Maybe it shouldn't have been—I was a PhD chemical engineer, and I probably should have figured that out already. At GE we coupled ideas with manufacturing disciplines. When a loan went bad, we worked it out; we didn't put a line through it. One business of ours, Polar Air, came about because we had leased a bunch of 747s to Pan Am, and the airline went out of business. We converted the planes to cargo carriers and started a shipping company. We got into the railcar business the same way, through a bankruptcy. That's what we could do at GE, because we had people with diverse operating experience, as well as capital, which gave us considerable staying power. (Collingwood and Coutu 2002)

When assigning each candidate to a business group, Jones and his EMS also set a target of 20 percent annual sales growth in their respective businesses for each candidate. Welch eventually succeeded Jones after a long, tough, competitive succession process. This would foster, rather strengthen, in this indomitable leader another value that he embodied in his previous organizational position, that is, using internal competition to train your managers and hone their skills.

CEO WELCH

When any of us assumes a new role, many thoughts go through our minds as to what we want to do. Our new Corporate Executive Office is having this experience, and we naturally have many objectives that, with the help of our great organization, we want to achieve.

But rather than talk about specific tasks, I want to reflect on what we want this Company to be in 1990—a decade from today—in two sentences.

We would like General Electric to be perceived as a unique, high-spirited, entrepreneurial enterprise, a company known around the world for its unmatched level of excellence. We want General Electric to be the most profitable, highly diversified company on earth, with world quality leadership in every one of its product lines—Welch in his first speech to GE shareholders in 1981. (GE Annual Report 1981)

Jack Welch acknowledged in his first speech to the shareholders at the annual meeting that he inherited a financially strong, well diversified, and internationalized company from his predecessor Reginald Jones. In fact he spent time in his speech talking about Jones' achievements as CEO of GE. He pointed out that GE was strong both technologically and financially and had made key R&D investments that positioned GE both strategically and financially for future growth. At the same time, however, he also noted a number of changes that were taking place in the environment and how GE needed to respond to those changes for it to be the most profitable company with world quality leadership in every one of its product lines. The Vice Chairman and then Senior Vice President and CFO Dennis Dammerman said in a lecture at Cornell University that the selection of Jack Welch, an unconventional candidate, was the single most riskiest leadership decision made by the then CEO Reginald Jones (Lakshman 2005). Specifically he said:

> Despite the eager availability of half a dozen highly talented and respected conventional candidates for CEO, he saw clearly the need for a faster, more energized, more growth-oriented GE. And, in an act of truly remarkable courage and foresight, he bet the Company on a 45-year-old anarchist named Jack Welch. (Dammerman 1998)

This "anarchist" started by asking for a revolution and getting one, although not overnight. He started breaking down the hierarchy and barriers in his quest for boundarylessness (the eventual label that would be applied to his philosophy of running GE). He kept repeating his vision of being No. 1 or No. 2 in every business that GE operates in and being better than the best, Welch's idea of excellence. Welch said to the shareholders in 1981, "To me, 'excellence' means being *better than the best*.'" Its achievement requires an introspective assessment of everything we do, say, or make, and an honest inquiry: "Is it 'better than the best'?" If it is not, we will ask ourselves, "What will it take?" and then rally the resources required to get there. If the economics or the environment determines that we can't get there, we must take the same spirited action to disengage ourselves from that which we can't make "better than the best." This was the seed for his idea of fixing, closing, or selling businesses that were not in the competitive position that Welch wanted it to be.

> In 1981, when we first defined our business strategy, the real focus was Japan. The entire organization had to understand that GE was in a tougher, more competitive world, with Japan as the cutting edge of the new competition. Nine years later, that competitive toughness has increased by a factor of five or ten. We face a revitalized Japan that's migrated around the world and responded successfully to a massive Yen change. So being number one or number two globally is more important than ever. (Tichy and Charan 1989: 15–34)

Welch started working first on this principle of being No. 1 or No. 2 by fixing, closing, and selling businesses for a period of five or so years. In the process he laid off more than 100,000 employees in a period of just four years. Not all of these were lost jobs though. Some of these jobs went along with the businesses to the buyers. In 1984, Fortune named him as one of the toughest bosses. Not everyone understood his vision of No. 1 or No. 2. Some did not understand the rationale behind the acquisitions and sale of businesses. "Why the heck is GE in the business of selling insurance (on the acquisition of Employers Reinsurance Inc.)? Why not invest US$1.1 billion in motors or lighting instead?" (*The Economist* 1991). GE was in financial services long before Jack Welch became CEO. Some executives had a clear understanding of Jack Welch's values of speed, self-confidence, information clarity, and excellence. They argued that Jack Welch was tough, but not unfair.

> The one thing that you can never do with Jack is wing it. If he catches you winging it, you're in trouble—real trouble. You have to go in with in-depth information. Stand up for what you believe, but acknowledge what you don't know when you don't know it. (Tichy and Charan 1989)

Thus, people who could get by in an earlier highly bureaucratic system with the protection of multiple layers of managers to corrupt the data and distort the information were really getting uncomfortable with Welch and his ideas. Through such institutions as the learning center at Crotonville, New York, GE and Welch had worked constantly on developing a values statement that could and would provide the rationale for the number of acquisitions and sell offs of businesses. Through an examination of internal GE documents, it became apparent that in 1985, the list of desired corporate values included those such as market leadership, above average returns from the businesses, the possession of a distinct competitive advantage, and operating in businesses that leverage GE's particular strengths—large scale, complex pursuits, that required massive capital investment in businesses that had staying power and in which GE had some managerial expertise (Tichy and Sherman 1992). Clearly, Jack Welch and his team of top managers had values and strategies consistent with strategic management thought to evolve much later, such as the concept of portfolio of core competencies developed by Hamel and Prahalad, reputed academicians/consultants.

The toughest boss story and the labeling of Welch as Neutron Jack was piling on the pressure on Welch and demanded Jack's response and he gave GE the RCA acquisition, labeled as the biggest coup ever pulled off. This served to provide a sense of identity to the thousands of GE employees who were upset with the sale of housewares and the acquisitions of insurance and other service businesses that seemed not to fit with GE's core businesses. RCA was originally a GE business that was sold to outsiders under pressure from antitrust actions. NBC, which came with RCA, also reestablished GE, albeit more strongly, in the television broadcasting business, which was also another business that GE had made earlier forays into.

Even before this grand coup, GE's financial performance had been grand. Through all the downsizing and sales and acquisitions, the company maintained a healthy profit margin. Sales grew from US$26.8 billion in 1980 to US$58.4 billion in 1990, an annual growth rate of over 8 percent and one-third better than inflation.

Profits in the same period grew by 11 percent a year, from US$1.5 billion to US$4.3 billion. Return on equity averaged nearly 19 percent a year. In the early 1990s Welch wanted to shift the focus in some areas and stay the course in others, as outlined in his initial speech to shareholders in 1981. Specifically Welch wanted GE to be an enterprise where (a) internal divisions blur and everyone works as a team, (b) suppliers and customers are partners, and (c) there is no segregation between foreign and domestic operations (*The Economist* 1991). Characterizing Welch's description of GE as a boundary-less company as awkward, *The Economist* listed the above-mentioned objectives, along with the countless other values emphasized earlier, all of which are consistent with more a recent concept, namely, Knowledge Management. In fact, Knowledge Management as a concept so characterizes Welch's approach to leading GE that he is the epitome of the concept.

KNOWLEDGE LEADERSHIP

Right from his days in the plastics industry, Welch continued to be an information junkie throughout the rest of his tenure as CEO. His decision-making methods had changed very little since his early days in plastics. He would gather together the people who had the relevant information, engage with them in a process of rigorous debate and tough questioning on the plans and the right decision to make, and when finally the decision was made, the people in the group owned the decision and were committed to it. The Corporate Executive Council (CEC) at GE is the embodiment of the concept of Knowledge Management. This was restricted to the top layer of GE's management. Jack Welch, not content with this level of openness, candor, and information movement, desperately wanted to move this deeper into the organization, and across the organizational boundaries to suppliers and customers. He designed the work-out, the organization-wide process of debate, discussion, and problem solving across all businesses of GE. Each business had its own executive council that mirrored the CEC in its knowledge sharing and managing functions that had significant business impact.

All of these mechanisms were also explicitly used to kill the *Not Invented Here* (NIH) syndrome, that bane of large organizations that get stuck in inertia. In his annual speech to shareholders in 2000 Welch remarked:

> A concept that has guided us for the better part of two decades is a belief that an organization's ability to learn, to transfer that learning across its components, and to act on it quickly is its ultimate, sustainable competitive advantage. That belief drove us to create a boundaryless company by delayering and destroying organizational silos. Selflessly sharing good ideas and endlessly searching for better ideas became a natural act. We purged NIH—not invented here—from our system, creating a company with an insatiable desire for information. All this was done the hard way, before the arrival of the Internet. Today, with the Internet, information is available everywhere to everyone, and a company that isn't searching for the best idea, isn't open to ideas from anywhere, will find itself left behind with its survival at stake. (*GE Annual Report* 2001)

The six-sigma initiative at GE was the result of a case study presentation made by former GE top executive and CEO of Allied Signal, Larry Bossidy. He had waxed on about the benefits of quality and the six-sigma approach founded by Motorola to the skeptical Welch that Welch invited him to make a presentation to GE executives in June 1995 at the CEC meeting in Crotonville. The presentation won rave reviews and Welch agreed to make the massive investments in training the tens of thousands of employees that the initiative would require. Although very expensive in terms of the monetary investment requirements, reportedly the savings in cost and productivity increases have gone way beyond the investments, with much of the costs being recouped by the benefits as early as 1997 (*GE Annual Report* 1998). The six-sigma initiative provides yet another instance of the knowledge sharing and learning approaches of Welch's leadership.

The Corporate Executive Council (CEC)

The council comprises 30 or so highest ranking executives (business chiefs) and meets for two days every quarter at the Crotonville learning center. The formal mandate of the CEC is to share information, swap ideas and transfer learning and knowledge from one business to others. The CEC was also conceived to be a high-level think tank that would solve key problems that arose in the different businesses that GE operated. These are highly informal meetings, with one implicit objective being the building of trust and increasing the familiarity of the business executives with each other. Welch said in one interview:

> These aren't stuffy, formal strategic reviews. We share ideas and information candidly and openly, including programs that have failed. The important thing is that at the end of these two days everyone in the CEC has seen and discussed the same information. The CEC creates a sense of trust, a sense of personal familiarity and mutual obligation at the top of the company. We consider the CEC a piece of organizational technology that is very important for our future success. (Tichy and Charan 1989: 15–32)

These council meetings were where Welch collected unfiltered information (in addition to the delayering attempts for a similar objective), tested and challenged his executives, and made sure that the organization's triumphs and failures were openly shared (Byrne 1998). The typical CEC session began with the CEO's overview of GE's current status and prospects along with a sounding of the big themes, such as globalization, cost reduction, productivity increases, and webifying businesses. This was followed by brief oral reports from the business leaders, with each of them lasting less than 10 minutes. The main agenda item was problem solving and transferring of best practices such as a new pay plan or a drug-testing program, or stock options, which by 1998 more than 27,000 employees had received at least once.[3] The CEC was also an expression of the values of candor and facing reality, which formed the core set of GE values under Welch.

> Every business is free to propose its own plan or program and present it at
> the CEC, and we put it through a central screen at corporate, strictly to make
> sure it's within the bounds of good sense. We don't approve the details.
> But we want to know what the details are so we can see which programs
> are working and immediately alert the other businesses to the successful
> ones. (Tichy and Sherman 1992)

The CEC concept is not limited to just the top executive levels. Welch first wanted the concept to flow down one level to the business leaders and their top executives from across functional areas within their business. He then took it organization wide with the work-out concept. At the level of each business, the business leaders created their own executive committee to meet on policy questions. This executive committee consists of members from across functional areas that get together every quarter for two days to function much like the corporate executive council. This resulted in people talking to each other across functions, helping them communicate with each other about their prospects and programs. It made people realize that their contributions count, that their ideas matter, and they could see that what they say and do is noticed and rewarded. In all of these councils, the guiding principles set forth by Welch are openness, candor, facing reality, and no-holds-barred debate. Welch wanted unfiltered information to be shared and discussed, which necessitated that these values were in place. Although these were highly effective sessions in building trust, increasing familiarity, transferring knowledge and learning, and in problem solving, Welch was not satisfied with the scale of these activities. He wanted much deeper penetration into the bowels of the organization and ensured that people at all levels participated in such sessions.

> We want 300,000 people with different career objectives, different family
> aspirations, different financial goals, to share directly in this company's vis-
> ion, the information, the decision-making process and the rewards. We want
> to build a more stimulating environment, a more creative environment,
> a freer work atmosphere, with incentives tied directly to what people do.
> (Tichy and Charan 1989: 15–32)

Enter the work-out.

Work-Out

By mid-1992, more than 200,000 GEers—well over two-thirds of the workforce—had experienced work-out. It is an ongoing process whereby on any given day about 20,000 employees may be engaged in the process of dialog with their managers about their work processes, productivity, and other issues that may concern them and their work places. In Welch's words:

> I want to get to a point where people challenge their bosses everyday: "Why do you require me to do these wasteful things? Why don't you let me do the things you shouldn't be doing so you can move on and create?" That's the job of a leader—to create, not to control. (Tichy and Sherman 1992)

Welch was actively involved in the process of work-out and going to every business to sit in on a work-out session. The purpose of his presence was not to question the ownership of the business, which Welch wanted the business leaders to have, but to ensure that the process was accepted and implemented well and was effective in bringing about change in the work processes for positive business results. Just as the vision of No.1 and No. 2 in each business took repeated communication and pushing, Welch thought that the work-out idea also needed such effort. Moreover, it permitted him and other top executives to identify and transfer knowledge from best units in terms of how they had understood and implemented the work-out process to other business units which were having trouble with it. Work-out was designed to deliver the Crotonville (John F. Welch Learning Center) experience to the great mass of GE employees as compared to the 10,000 people per year that were part of the elite corporate population who went to Crotonville. Building trust was one of the basic goals of the work-out process, where GE employees could discover that they could speak out as candidly as members of the corporate executive council, without jeopardizing their careers. Only then would GE get the benefit of employees' best ideas and would truly be sharing or managing knowledge. One of the other objectives is to eliminate unnecessary work, much of which remained and eluded the delayering and restructuring attempts by Welch, in the form of unnecessary reports, filling out countless forms, and taking superfluous measurements. The broader quest was for improved productivity. Another objective of the work-out, in Welch's words:

> The other thing we want to achieve, the intellectual part, begins by putting the leaders of each business in front of 100 or so of their people, eight to 10 times a year, to let them hear what their people think about the company, what they like, what they don't like about their work, about how they're evaluated, about how they spend their time. Work-out will expose the leaders to the vibrations of their business—opinions, feelings, emotions, resentments, not abstract theories of organization and management.[4]

Work-out began in October of 1988 under the guidance of Jim Baughman and his Crotonville team. The early stage was a series of local gatherings patterned after New England town meetings. In groups of 30 to 100, the hourly and salaried employees of a particular business would spend three days at an off-site conference center discussing their common problems. Dress was casual. The setting and behavior was unusual. To ensure that people could speak candidly without fearing retribution, bosses were locked out during discussion times. Welch made it clear to business leaders that he would treat any obstruction of work-out as "a career limiting move." Facilitators, all outside consultants at first, ran the sessions. Meeting in small groups, the employees would define the problems and develop concrete proposals. On the final day, the bosses would return. According to work-out's rules, they had to make instant, on-the-spot decisions about each proposal, and right in front of everyone. This kind of a process is highly similar to what happened at the Learning Center, groups of thousands of middle managers working on problems and presenting proposals to senior executives. Some 80 percent of the proposals in the initial stages of the introduction of work-out got immediate yes-no decisions. The rest that needed study had to get decided within a month. As Welch had hoped, the process quickly exposed managers who did not walk the talk.

Even though people spent much of the early work-out sessions griping, managers recount countless instances of how the process worked. At one plant, a manager said:

> We were getting screws from one supplier that were not so good. The bits would break off the screw heads, and scratch the product, and our people's hands—we had one guy get 18 stitches. Tempers flared, but management never fixed the problem. They said, "OK, we'll get you some screws from the good supplier." But the bad screws would always reappear. So a shop steward named Jimmy stood up at work-out and told the story. This guy was a maverick, a naysayer. He wanted to test us to see whether we really wanted change. He knew what he was talking about. And he explained the solution, which had to do with how deep the bit could be inserted into the screw head.... We need to go tell the supplier what the problems are. Well, I was nervous about it, but I decided to charter a plane to fly Jimmy and a couple of other guys to the plant in Virginia where they made the bad screws. They left that very night. Jimmy got that problem fixed and it sent a powerful signal to everyone here. He became a leader instead of a maverick. (Tichy and Sherman 1992)

External Benchmarking

To supplement the work-outs, Welch developed the global best practices program. GE's team scoured the world for companies which were better than GE at some specific aspect of business and then asked to pick their brains. In return GE promised to share with them the knowledge it gained. Nine companies worldwide were picked including Ford, HP, American Express, Digital Equipment, and Honda. The case studies developed by each of these teams became part of the curriculum at Crotonville (*The Economist* 1991). This process of external benchmarking is the one that is the most obvious component of Welch's leadership centered on Knowledge Management. The best practices programs and the associated teams were intertwined with the work-out process so much to be almost inseparable. The six-sigma initiative with its massive benefits in cost savings, productivity increase, and innovations were the result of such benchmarking. In addition, however, because the six-sigma initiative required thousands of personnel to be trained in methods, statistics, and so on, it represented another means of knowledge management through such efforts as management development and training and development.

The Six-Sigma Initiative

Welch came late to this rigorous, statistical approach to quality control, for he was skeptical about the approach and criticized it for being heavy on slogans and light on results. Welch launched the effort in late 1995 with 200 projects and intensive training programs, moved to 3,000 projects and more training in 1996, and undertook 6,000 projects and still more training in 1997. More than 100,000 people had been trained in the quality process methodology in early 2000. A *Business Week* article reports that in the last three years alone (as of 2002), the trained teams of employees have saved the company some US$8 billion compared to his objective and belief in the company's ability to achieve about US$5 billion in savings by the year 2000 (Arndt 2002 and Byrne 1998). Very briefly, Six-Sigma means going from 35,000 errors per million operations or 35,000 defects per million products produced (three sigma)—which is the average for most companies—to just under four defects (3.4 per million), Six-Sigma, in operations as wide ranging as the production of locomotives to the handling of mortgage applications. The Six-Sigma approach involves reducing the defects and making the process as perfect as possible and controlling the process to maintain that level of perfection. The financial returns from Six-Sigma, although exceeding expectations, is only one part of the story, with billions more to be captured from increased volume and market share as customers increasingly "feel" the benefits of GE Six-Sigma in their own businesses. Welch reported in his 1999 speech to shareholders:

> We are now beginning to see the first major products **designed** for Six Sigma production, designed in effect by the customer, incorporating every feature he or she considers critical to quality.

The first major Six Sigma-designed product to reach the market—the LightSpeed, a multislice CT scanner—reached our customers in 1998. This lifesaving machine is revolutionizing medical diagnostics. A chest scan that takes a conventional scanner three minutes to perform takes 17 seconds with LightSpeed. A full body scan for a trauma patient, for whom speed can mean life or death, now takes 32 seconds when a conventional scanner could take ten minutes or longer. I brought the tape of the ceremony that marked its introduction.

We've shown that tape to every single senior manager in this Company because it represents the future, when **every** product in this company will be designed for Six Sigma and **every** customer will be as delighted as those doctors are.[5]

Thus, in one swoop, Welch combined knowledge management with quality and innovation, while enhancing customer responsiveness.

The other aspects of Welch's leadership role at GE centered on information and knowledge management include the Crotonville center, which was founded and established in the 1950s by CEO Ralph Cordiner. The delayering and restructuring aimed at moving information much faster than before through the organization, and most importantly, the technology component of knowledge management in the form of information systems and e-business initiatives. At Crotonville, the norm used to be to train and develop the managers based on the blue books, which Welch scorned. Managers were brought to the learning center in truckloads and trained in POIM: Plan, Organize, Integrate, and Measure. In contrast, through the same institution of Crotonville and through other things such as the work-out, Welch wanted his managers to liberate, trust, debate, and act. Much like the work-out where hourly, salaried, and much of the lower level employees worked on concrete proposals and presented them for approval to their bosses, at Crotonville, middle level managers and top executives worked on such concrete proposal building, presenting, and obtaining approval on projects. In addition, they would enroll in training courses conducted by faculty members from reputed universities and by top internal executives including Welch, a frequent teacher at the institute. The CEC always met at the Crotonville learning center. In addition, the top 500 or so executives met every year in

Boca Raton, Florida, to celebrate successes and share knowledge on a number of initiatives such as the Six-Sigma program. Amid palms and ocean breezes, Jack Welch used the opportunity to set the agenda for the coming year and to recognize the heroes of the previous year. Being invited to this annual session was the equivalent of winning the Olympic gold medal for most managers. The show-and-tell routine allows managers in the plastics sector to exchange lessons with their counterparts in GE Capital. It's a place, like Croton-on-Hudson, where "best practices" get transferred among GE's differing businesses. In between sessions, managers who make bulbs or locomotives swap ideas with those who finance cars and service credit-card accounts.

The delayering he undertook in eliminating the entire top layer of top managers was also in the effort to eliminate information distortion, and increase the speed of business decision-making with faster movement of information. The other benefits of the delayering were (a) far fewer time-consuming requests for information, (b) less time spent in the informal review process, (c) much faster decision-making, and (d) quicker, clearer communication.

The Technology Dimension of Welch's Knowledge Leadership

As early as 1993, GE information services had instituted systems that electronically graded GE services to its customers and provided a daily report card (*Financial World* 1993). Much like his other initiatives, Welch did not believe in half-measures and went full force into the e-business initiative at GE. Welch mandated that GE turn itself into an e-business in January 1999, soon after his wife introduced him to the net (McGinn 2000 and Levinson 2000). To kick its e-business initiative into high gear, Welch devised a technique through which he asked his unit chiefs to figure out how to save their businesses by determining how to kill them, the Destroy Your Business (DYB) exercise. This was followed by the Build Your Business (BYB) exercise, under the guidance of the CIO Gary Reiner and the general managers of the e-business initiative for each of the businesses. In his speech to shareholders in 2000 Welch said of his longstanding value of *reality*:

> Seeing reality today means accepting the fact that e-Business is here. It's not coming. It's not the thing of the future. It's here. Reality today means "go on offense." One cannot be tentative about this. Excuses like channel conflict, or "marketing and sales aren't ready," or "the customers aren't prepared" cannot be allowed to divert or paralyze the offensive. Moving aggressively raises some thorny issues with no clear and immediate solutions, but the challenge is to resolve these issues on the fly in the context of the new Internet reality. Tentativeness in action can mean being cut out of markets, perhaps not by traditional competitors but by companies never heard of 24 months ago.[6]

Welch and GE have been so aggressive with this initiative that *Internet Week* recently named GE as America's top e-business. GE's web enabled systems provide such benefits to internal customers by sharing knowledge with suppliers and to external customers by sharing their own design and product knowledge with them that these systems more than adequately reach the 1991 Welchian goal of boundarylessness, where Welch conceived of knocking down walls that separate units and create divisions between the organization and the suppliers and customers on the outside. Welch wanted all of these divisions to blur and create a seamless system in which customers and suppliers would be partners. The system created at GE plastics, for example, provides new tools that let product engineers get a sense of which materials they should use and how much they will cost. For example, a product engineer at a cell phone manufacturer plugs the dimensions of her product into GE Plastics' system and selects four different materials she's interested in using. GE's system then helps her determine how many molds she has to build to make a part. When she's done in a few hours, she has a fairly extensive matrix of what products would work and a ballpark figure on costs. It gives her an enormous head start on the process of designing the product (Levinson 2000). In appliances, the installation of Point-of-Sale (POS) terminals at retailers like Home Depot enables customers to enter selections, preferences for delivery, and so on, and eventually have the product delivered to their homes and installed. The retailer gets a cut on the sale and stays very happy. At medical systems, the e-business initiative helps in such areas as facilitating the downloading of software by doctors and technicians to run their Magnetic Resonance Imaging (MRI) systems on a trial basis and then buy if they so desire. Numerous applications such as these help GE in managing knowledge, facilitating transactions with customers and suppliers, and thereby enhancing profitability, much more so than the oft-quoted cost reduction functions of such systems (Rudnitsky 2000).

Through all these years one thing that has characterized Welch is his consistency of thoughts, values, and ideas, in addition to his focus on continuous improvement through such processes as the work-out. Although not completely enamored by the Japanese concept of *Kaizen* and the related incremental change, this firm believer of quantum change did, however, realize the value of incremental and continuous improvement. Welch expressed his views on consistency as follows:

> You don't get anywhere if you keep changing your ideas. The only way to change people's minds is with consistency. Once you get the ideas, you keep refining and improving them. The more simply your idea is defined, the better it is. You communicate, you communicate, and then you communicate some more. Consistency, simplicity, and repetition are what it's all about...we never changed, we just got better at it. And after a while it started to snowball. (Tichy and Charan 1989)

In addition to his consistency of ideas and values and the specific realm of Knowledge Management oriented leadership activities such as the CEC, learning center, work-out, boundarylessness, and so on, Welch also embodied a very personal side of knowledge management. Every week, he made unexpected visits to plants and offices, hurriedly scheduled luncheons with managers several layers below him, and sent countless handwritten notes to GE people that suddenly churned off their fax machines, revealing his bold yet neat handwriting. All of it was meant to lead, guide, and influence the behavior of a complex organization. Welch knew by sight the names and responsibilities of at least the top 1,000 people at GE. He knew their names. He knew what they did. That's an incredible reinforcement to the individual that he or she counts. Welch was also known for writing personal notes to communicate with employees and managers at all levels in the organization. His handwritten notes, faxed to different target employees as appreciatory gestures, acknowledging excellent work, expressing gratitude, following up on ongoing work, and providing timely feedback had great impact on its targets. His belief in creating a personal touch and his immense belief in the power of the individual's efficiency/creativity was unbounded. "The idea flow from the human spirit is absolutely unlimited," Welch declares. "All you have to do is tap into that well. I don't like to use the word efficiency. It's creativity. It's a belief that every person counts" (Byrne 1998). It was, perhaps, because of this belief that Welch also believed in standing up for and supporting his people, especially when he had spent so much time and energy finding the best people, which he did consistently. He expressed it thus, "A manager's job is to make his people feel ten feet tall-strong, powerful, self-confident, willing to take risks. Running down your own team is one of the worst things a leader can do" (Collingwood and Coutu 2002). He also believed in putting the best people in positions where they were required. More importantly he thought that one needs to put better people in positions than the positions seem to deserve at the time. "If it's a US$5 million business, put a US$300 million person to work on it while it's still US$5 million, and they'll make it US$300 million. You put a US$5 million person on it, and it'll stay US$5 million" (Collingwood and Coutu 2002). Although GE's success is hardly Welch's alone, no other CEO has added so much value to their organization in terms of market capitalization as Welch has. GE has always boasted of its rich managerial talent and having been a top executive at GE was often listed as a qualification for a CEO position in many companies. Many former GE executives run successful organizations as CEOs (Gross 2003), although not all of them are successful in their respective positions. The wealth of talent at GE is limitless and the credit for turning around each of the businesses needs to be spread around to the scores of executives that have worked in the bowels of this organization to turnaround productivity, quality, and customer responsiveness of their individual businesses. However, Welch still deserves a lion's share of that credit, as his values became core corporate values for the organization and for others who also benchmarked and imitated GE approaches. While analysts on Wall Street or GE's own investors view Welch's likely legacy as creating the world's most valuable company in stock market terms, Welch himself sees things quite differently. The man who spent more than 50 percent of his time on people issues considers the care and feeding of talent his greatest achievement. "This place runs by its great people," said Welch. "The biggest accomplishment I've had is to find great people. An army of them. They are all better than most CEOs. They are big hitters, and they seem to thrive here" (Byrne 1998).

NOTES

1. Welch uses the word "staying power" to refer to his choice of businesses in several interviews, for example, Tichy and Charan (1989: 15–32).
2. See implicit theories of leaders in Lord and Maher (1991), and cause-effect beliefs in Burns (1978).
3. Dennis Dammerman, Durland Memorial Lecture, Cornell University, April 1, 1998.
4. Letter to Shareholders, *GE Annual Report* 1989.
5. Speech to shareholders at the Annual Stockholders meeting, 1999. See *GE Annual Report* 1999.
6. Speech to shareholders at the Annual Stockholders meeting, 2000. See *GE Annual Report* 2000.

8

INDIAN KNOWLEDGE LEADERSHIP

Y.C. DEVESHWAR AND E-CHOUPALS

e-choupal goes beyond mere knowledge-connectivity and enables farmers to exercise the informed choice by connecting them to local and global markets. Thus, the human and the digital infrastructure at the village is complemented and completed with a physical infrastructure in the form of 'Choupal Saagars', each at the center of a cluster of 40 e-choupals. Saagars offer multiple services under one roof— a marketing platform, store front for agri-equipment and personal consumption products, insurance counters, pharmacy & health center, agri-extension clinic, fuel station and a food court.... ITC has innovated a win-win situation for the farmers and the shareholders of ITC by linking the farm operations directly to their agri-export business through e-choupal. The system has avoided the middlemen and also ensured quality product reaching the national and international markets with quality certification needed by the importing countries.

—Dr A.P.J. Abdul Kalam
(Special address during the National Symposium
to commemorate 60 years of independence, 2007.)

India is one of the rare countries of the world where the knowledge economy operates side-by-side with an industrial and an agrarian economy, each of these operating on its own rules of business (see Table 8.1). This, as stated in an early chapter, is one of the huge challenges offered by emerging economies such as India. India's rural market, more specifically, is a potentially huge market at 720 million consumers (>70 percent of population), however, constituting less than 30 percent of the country's Gross Domestic Product (GDP). Adding to the problem of small wallets, the rural market is also characterized by high-levels of dispersion and unsustainable population densities for the marketer. The farmer's plight is no less, in that land ownership is dispersed and fragmented (average 1.5 hectares), plagued with weak infrastructure, heavily dependent on the monsoon, and the presence of numerous intermediaries. If you look at this picture and see the tremendous opportunity for integrating, sharing, leveraging, and managing information and converting it into a business model, you would be on par with the ITCs of the world and visionaries such as Y.C. Deveshwar, Chairman of Indian Tobacco Company (ITC). According to G. Ramachandran, a financial analyst and member of the Shankerlal Guru Committee on agricultural markets, e-choupal has correctly regarded India's agrarian and rural poverty as the result of a cruel situation faced by India's small and poor farmers, which forces them to operate and transact in 'un-evolved' markets. Farmers and rural households remain uninformed or inadequately informed in these 'un-evolved' markets because of adverse societal and economic structures (*Business Line* 2005).

Fighting against a conventional wisdom in the western world of focusing on one core business, in a situation where 33 percent of the company (ITC) is owned by British American Tobacco (BAT), a British tobacco behemoth, Chairman Y.C. Deveshwar wanted to excel in several: other consumer goods besides tobacco, such as flour, cooking oil, matches, and salt, hotels, paper, paperboard and packaging, and agribusiness—the source of e-choupals (*The Economist* 2004). Arguing that the concept of focus is a western

Table 8.1
GDP by Sector

Macroeconomic indicators	1993	1998	1999	2000	2001	2002	2007
Nominal GDP (measured in thousand of US$)	273.93	414.32	444.35	450.68	481.42	500.99	695.78
Agricultural (% of GDP)	28.16	25.42	23.85	22.74	22.76	23.15	19.60
Industry (% of GDP)	23.88	24.33	23.53	24.23	23.59	26.35	30.60
Services (% of GDP)	38.90	42.05	43.59	44.16	44.85	50.50	49.90

Source: University of Michigan Business School Case Study on e-choupal (The Economic Intelligence Unit).

fixation, Deveshwar has gone on to create strategies for ITC in a multi-business environment. The ITC group of companies is one of India's largest private sector companies with a market capitalization of approximately US$ 4 billion and annual sales of US$ 2 billion. In a context within which the organization was concerned about social responsibility, triple bottom line reporting, and national development, Deveshwar and his team of executives developed the concept of the e-choupal that could integrate, leverage, share, and manage information in a fragmented and dispersed rural marketplace. The overall objective of the organization is to balance investor interests with those of the communities in which they operate and that of the government. The creation of a business model for development within the context of the international business division (US$150 million in revenues), an agricultural trading company provided the immediate context for the e-choupal. The e-choupal was simultaneously conceived as a more efficient solution for the company's supply chain as well an e-commerce platform for selling the company's goods and services to farmers.

The e-choupals were established as a business platform consisting of a set of organizational subsystems and interfaces with the potential of connecting farmers to global markets (*Business Line* 2007a). The purpose of establishing such an organizational system leveraging IT infrastructure was to utilize the structure in both procurement of supplies from the farmers and for providing a host of services and products to them as consumers. The e-choupal business platform consists of three broad layers. The first layer consists of the village level kiosks with internet access (e-choupal), managed by an ITC trained local farmer called a *sanchalak*. These choupals are located within walking distance of each target farmer, with approximately one e-choupal located per cluster of five villages. The second layer consists of a bricks and mortar infrastructure called "hubs" managed by the traditional intermediary who has local knowledge and skills. This person, a former commission agent in the traditional *mandi* system, which the e-choupal system partly substituted, is called a *samyojak*. The *samyojak* in this second layer is located within the premises of a large mall targeting the rural farmers and their families. These malls called *Choupal Sagars*, are spread over 7,000 square feet and stock all the leading brands of clothes, home appliances, other consumer goods, and a variety of farm related supplies needed by the farmer like fertilizers, pumps, pesticides, and so on. The third layer consists of the various product and service providers, in addition to ITC itself as the procurer of farm output.

Today the e-choupal initiative comprises 6400 choupals transforming the lives of over 3.5 million farmers, in 38,500 villages in nine states of India. By 2010, the company has set target coverage of 20,000 choupals for 10 million farmers in 100,000 villages transacting US$2.5 billion in business.[1] At the end of 2005, there were about 50 *Choupal Sagars* spread over four states, with more planned for the other states.

The e-choupal business platform is an excellent illustration of the knowledge transfer and utilization mechanisms at work. The computer with internet access located within a *sanchalak*'s home becomes the means through which ITC channels information and knowledge in a number of different domains to the farmers. This information and knowledge ranges from daily prices for grains and crops at the *mandi* (the traditional outlet for sale of grains), to weather information, information on cropping practices, and healthcare information, in addition to the open information available on the internet. For instance, *sanchalaks* have been known to use the system to track prices at the local *mandi* as well as to track prices on the Chicago commodities exchange. The use of trained *sanchalaks*, local farmers with local knowledge and skills, forms a key constituent of the reverse movement of information and knowledge from the villages to the multinational corporation (ITC). The same system can be used as a two-way transaction processing system for the farmers to sell their output to ITC and to use it to order a variety of supplies they themselves require for use in their farms or households. The need of the day for both the farmers and for ITC and a variety of rural marketers was disintermediation. The numerous intermediaries in the Indian rural markets have a history of earning trading profits by undermining the structure and magnitude of rewards accruing to poor farmers owning small tracts of land (Ramchandran 2004). The system was such that the farmers were not getting an adequate price for their output, while at the same time the consumers were not getting their produce for a fair price. The intermediaries were blocking information and market signals and using these activities as the basis of their profit making. Thus, the movement of information and knowledge, sharing knowledge between the producer and the value-adding intermediaries such as the food processing companies, and leveraging of such knowledge would benefit all the people in the value-chain. Understanding the motivations and vested interests of the *mandi* traders, and using many of them as *samyojaks*, was a stroke of genius on ITC's part, although not completely without resistance. In December 2004, Soyabean trading at the *mandis* in Madhya Pradesh came to a grinding halt as a result of an indefinite strike observed by the traders in various locations (*Business Line* 2004c). The strike was in protest of the e-choupal direct marketing system. With much more information about price trends, the farmers were holding on to their produce waiting for better prices, lowering trade volumes in the *mandis*, and leading to the stir among traders. Farmers are able to make better decisions about whom to sell their output to and at what price, not to mention their decision-making ability in planting, irrigation, and other cropping practices as a result of the increased information flows made available to them.

It is a win-win situation from the perspective of ITC. It has craftily invested its time and effort in the multilayered organizational system, under the able knowledge leadership of Deveshwar, to obtain valuable information from the farmers, offer them prices for their output at prevailing market levels, in addition to using the system to sell them a bundle of products and services, in coordination with about 80 or so corporations. ITC has hooked up with Intellect, the research and technologies wing of the Lintas Media group to launch Bharat barometer—the primary informa-tion source on all aspects of rural consumer behavior (*Business Line* 2006b). Sivakumar, CEO of ITC International Business Division says:

> The enthusiastic response from farmers has encouraged us to plan for the extension of the e-choupal initiative to 11 other states across India over the next few years. There are plans to channelise services related to micro-credit, insurance, health and education through the same e-choupal infrastructure. (*Business Line* 2004b)

Having established the rural information infrastructure highway, the company is in wait of other potential users who are in plenty: state governments putting their services online, consumer-goods firms, whose distribution networks rarely get to the smaller vil-lages, microcredit providers, and so on. Deveshwar jubilantly said, "We will be owners of the road and, of course, we will charge a toll" (*The Economist* 2004). Attesting to the success of ITC's e-choupal initiative, a few other firms are planning to roll out simi-lar initiatives.

THE VILLAGE LEVEL

The internet-connected computer is usually housed within the *sanchalak*'s house and the connectivity is through either a phone line or through a satellite connection. Each of these choupals serves approximately 600 farmers located in five to ten nearby villages, with ITC aiming (strategic intention) to ultimately provide one such location within five kilometers of any farmer in rural India. Each of these choupals takes an approximate investment by ITC of 2 lakh rupees, and yearly operating and maintenance costs borne by the *sanchalak*, who receives a commission in return for his 'aggregating' services. The *sanchalak* also receives a certain level of social prestige as a result of being selected, hired, and trained by a multinational corporation. ITC channels all its communications through the *sanchalaks*, knowing fully well that the farmer has historically been taken advantage of and that trust is a very critical element in any transaction for the villagers. All *sanchalaks* take a public oath vouching for their actions benefiting the village community. Understanding that trust is a critical element of all knowledge sharing activities, the effective knowledge leadership of ITC builds its core knowledge network component (village choupal) by carefully selecting and training the individual who runs it. All *sanchalaks* are selected for their ability to communicate, build trust by virtue of actions and status, literacy, willingness to try new things, risk taking ability, and availability. In addition to accessing daily closing prices, the farmers use the e-choupal to order seeds, fertilizers, and consumer goods from ITC or its partners. At the time of harvest, ITC usually offers to buy the crop at the previous day's closing price. Farmers willing to sell at that price transport their goods to the ITC processing center (in many cases the *Choupal Sagar*), where the produce is electronically weighed (a process subject to farmer complaints and pilferage in the traditional *mandi* system) and assessed for quality. Farmers get their price and a transport fee. Thus, the farmers minimize on transaction costs, which would otherwise go to the intermediary with added margins. Some farmers do sell directly to the crushers (in the case of soyabean) and others still sell their produce at the *mandi*—the traditional system set up to enable farmers to get the best prices—which has ended up benefiting the traders more than the farmers.

THE *CHOUPAL SAGAR*

When the farmers collect their money at the *Choupal Sagar*, they are physically located tantalizingly close to the shopping aisles of the mall, with complete access to a line of products from motorcycles to fertilizers, branded clothes to farm equipment, and from diesel to home appliances, with Automated Teller Machines (ATMs) and other outsourced retailers lined up to participate. The intention is to capitalize on both the impulsive and planned buying habits of farmers and their families. However, the farmer stands to benefit by being provided the transportation costs for bringing the crop to the warehouse located at the *Choupal Sagar*, and by not being cheated in the process of weighing and assessing quality. The combined system of buying and selling provides sufficient levels of checks and balances to motivationally ensure that such defrauding does not take place. Moreover, the *samyojaks* running the *Choupal Sagars*, although disadvantaged as traders in the traditional *mandi* system, are now part of the value-chain run by a larger entity, the multinational corporation. They provide the bridge financing by paying the farmers and later collecting it from ITC. They manage storage transportation, and other logistics for a commission. Many *mandi* traders have agreed to work as *samyojaks* as a combined result of a desire to work for a global company and the fragmented nature of the *mandi* agents, with some level of competition amongst themselves. These *samyojaks* provide the working capital as against the major infrastructure investment provided by ITC for the mall, the warehouse, and the electronic infrastructure. Such investment also sends powerful signals to the traders that they are dealing with a significantly powerful entity in the business. In the end, it seems like a win-win situation for all. The *samyojaks* are another crucial element in the information and knowledge-leveraging network component of the e-choupal. They bring in their years of experience of handling the system and are able to provide crucial inputs on markets and trends to the e-choupal system. In return for taking an agent's role versus the earlier principal's role, the *samyojak* benefits by managing the mall, selling consumer goods, household provisions, etc., and by finding work for him and his staff throughout the year rather than just during the harvest season.

The dynamics of the e-choupal system, including the powerful motivating features of the traditional system and the alternative e-choupal system provide an excellent illustration of the Knowledge Leadership at work, similar to the motivational problems faced by Toyota's knowledge sharing network discussed in chapter six. Toyota had to face such motivational issues among its network of suppliers, eventually owing the success of its supplier knowledge-sharing network to its excellent management of the multifaceted motivational challenges.

ITC AND PROVIDERS OF PRODUCTS AND SERVICES

The *Choupal Sagars* stock the products of about 80 companies who pay a fee to ITC for using the channel to reach the difficult to reach rural consumer (*Businessline* 2004a). The fee serves as a toll on the "road" of the physical infrastructure built by ITC. A similar possibility for charging toll exists in the virtual realm as well for direct sales through the e-choupal, which are serviced through the *Choupal Sagars* acting as warehouses, thereby forming a clicks and mortar infrastructure. All the providers of products and services benefit by leveraging the physical infrastructure built by one company over the offerings of all the companies, thereby bringing down distribution costs. ITC benefits because it can get better quality delivered at its doorstep at better prices compared to the conventional option of obtaining grains from the *mandi*. Sivakumar, CEO of ITC-IBD gives the example of Aashirvaad Atta in explaining the success of the e-choupal system. He said:

> If under two years ITC's Aashirwad aata (flour) has become the No. 1 brand in the country with nearly 15 percent of the market share, it is because of quality, which is the result of the choupal infrastructure. We now buy from the farmer directly and are able to store different varieties of wheat separately. When farmers sell in mandis or the FCI, all the wheat gets aggregated. And after that it can't be segregated. So sometimes the aata

quality is very good, sometimes it is quite bad, and the consumer has to deal with it. But today when we store wheat separately, we have different blends. What is sold in Kolkata, Mumbai, or Chennai is very different as consumer preference is different in terms of level of coarseness, colour, usage patterns, the water absorption capacity, and so on. Earlier consumer preferences were not matched with the wheat grown, and the farmer didn't get the right value for his produce. But that is changing now. (*Business Line* 2004a)

Thus, as can be seen, the process of creating, sharing, and leveraging information extends all the way from the farmer to the consumer as a result of the e-choupal system, thereby making it an excellent illustration of the concept of Knowledge Leadership along the entire value-chain. The company is working on traceability of farm produce aimed at adding value by providing buyers products of their choice. Traceability is the ability to track the origin of a product and its attributes. Such a feature would help add value and get higher returns to farmers. Traceability is extended to some produce, aquaculture products backed by insurance, and fruits. The concept of traceability adds to the value of information and knowledge of sources of products and the resulting value in the marketplace. Wheat from Punjab and some parts of Madhya Pradesh are valued more than other sources and rice from certain locations are more valuable than others. The e-choupal network leverages this fact by helping identify and track the source of various products, which would otherwise not be possible under the traditional system, with the intermediaries oftentimes muddling that information and blocking signals. Seeing the potential value of the choupal systems, more and more companies are aligning themselves with ITC in their efforts to reach the rural consumer, thereby enhancing the efficacy of the e-choupal network and further lowering distribution costs. Motorola India recently joined the growing list of companies that are aiming to use the retail space provided within the e-choupal network. Dukes Consumer Care Ltd, a Hyderabad based confectionery maker also recently tied up with ITC to market its products through the e-choupal network. Direct To Home (DTH) player Tata Sky is another company that has recently tied up with ITC's e-choupal initiative to reach the rural areas and expand its business. All this is only likely to bring more consumerism to the people in the rural areas and bring economic benefits to all the participants.

ITC has won the Development Gateway Award, the Tata Energy Research Institute (TERI) Award, and the Golden Peacock Award for its e-choupal initiative, all serving to illustrate the value of the e-choupal network and the knowledge leadership strongly behind it. The Development Gateway Foundation recognized ITC's initiative in giving farmers access to market information with a US$100,000 award called the Development Gateway Award 2005. Chairman Deveshwar said:

> By delivering essential healthcare and educational information, we can extend the benefits of e-choupal more deeply into the fabric of our communities across India. And by recognizing programmes like ours, the Development Gateway Foundation is spurring on the use of information technologies in communities worldwide, to build grassroots capacities and enhance the quality of life. (*Appropriate Technology* 2005)

The foundation based in Washington DC, with operations in 60 countries, puts the internet to work for developing countries and helps improve lives by enabling more effective development worldwide. Awards such as this serve also to attest to the efficacy of such initiatives and of effective knowledge leadership in this context. Imitation is the best form of flattery. When other organizations such as the National Alliance on Mission 2007 also aim to create a massive network of information kiosks in six lakh villages in India by August 2007, acknowledging the importance of "village knowledge centers", nothing more is required to validate this knowledge leadership initiative. "Village knowledge centre (VKC) is one of the essential components for realizing our goal of graduating into a knowledge society," said Dr A.P.J. Abdul Kalam, speaking at the second annual convention of the National Alliance.

In addition, the company has also been bestowed with 2004 Corporate Social Responsibility Award from TERI for its e-choupal initiative. The award provides impetus to sustainable development and encourages ongoing social responsibility processes within the corporate sector. The company's social responsibility initiatives (e-choupal and social and farm forestry) were also recognized with the award of the Golden Peacock Global Award for social responsibility in Emerging Economies for 2005. The award was presented to the company in London by Dr Ola Ullsten, former Prime Minister of Sweden, who headed the jury. Capping it all is the induction of the chairman Y.C. Deveshwar into the "Hall of Pride" by the Indian Science Congress.

The business goals served by the company's e-choupal initiative should not be lost on the readers. Given that more organizations, both in the private and public sector (including some Non-Governmental Organizations [NGOs]), are mimicking the e-choupal initiative for rural marketing and development objectives, respectively, it should be clear that such initiatives achieve a great blend of both kinds of objectives. Conceiving of the problem as one that requires the management of information and knowledge, thereby sharing, integrating, and leveraging knowledge, is the first critical step in the knowledge leadership process illustrated by Deveshwar and his team. Utilizing local farmers as *sanchalaks*, and making them take public oath as though they were occupying a public office, serves as a crucial element building trust in the farming community. The utilization of the system without this trust would have been highly in doubt. Managing motivational challenges of other key stakeholders in the process, namely, the commission agents (traders) in the traditional *mandi* system serves as the other crucial element in the building of the socio-cognitive network of knowledge, a crucial requirement of knowledge leadership initiatives as outlined in an earlier chapter. The strength of vision possessed by the team of leaders in overcoming the many infrastructure difficulties (lack of power, lack of bandwidth) and other obstacles, in the face of potential returns not coming through, is another critical element of the knowledge leadership initiative. The balancing of both the technological and socio-cognitive knowledge networks and channelizing them for optimum effectiveness is another critical feature of this initiative, again as specified in an earlier chapter. The utilization of knowledge network in managing both the supply side and the distribution side of the value-chain is perhaps the uniqueness of this knowledge leadership initiative.

NOTE

1. Chairman Y.C. Deveshwar's address at ITC's 96th Annual General Meeting, July 27, 2007.

9

GLOBAL KNOWLEDGE LEADERSHIP

PERCY BARNEVIK'S MATRIX MANAGEMENT AT ABB

We rotate people around the world. There is no substitute for line experience in 3 or 4 countries to create a global perspective.... You also encourage people to work in mixed-nationality teams. You force them to create personal alliances across borders."

"ABB is an organization with 3 internal contradictions. We want to be global and local, big and small, radically decentralized with centralized reporting and control.... That's where the matrix comes in....

—Percy Barnevik, former CEO of ABB
(In an interview with William Taylor, *HBR*, 1991)

P erhaps the biggest phenomenon to affect businesses and their leaders is that of globalization. It is no longer sufficient to operate in and find strength in one's own domestic market. The history of the last 30 years or so is replete with the failures of businesses that have tried the one country approach. With the rampant growth in cross-border mergers and acquisitions, the globalization trend is becoming more acute than ever. In combination with the economic transition from an industrial age to the information age, the globalization phenomenon has made the lives of business leaders around the world much more complex. Nowhere else is the need for new types of leadership as imperative as it is in the globalized context. Managers dealing with a few countries now have to deal with dozens of countries, if not dozens regional groupings of countries. Neither *global* nor *multidomestic* strategies are sustainable in the long run in today's economic context. The transnational corporation has firmly arrived on the global scene complete with the challenging task of integrating and rationalizing the operations of these firms across countries. This challenging task places such a huge information load on the managers running these operations that it becomes imperative to search for new solutions. Some corporations and their charismatic CEOs, such as ABB and Percy Barnevik have blazed new trails, however temporarily, in accomplishing success in their fight against this huge challenge. To be sure, ABB has achieved tremendous success under its capable knowledge leader Percy Barnevik, collapsed in the aftermath of his exit, and has been strongly on the revival path since its collapse. The swings in the fortunes of ABB simply suggest that the knowledge leadership attempt of Percy Barnevik, utilizing a matrix organizational structure, which was once hailed as a model for global management of businesses, needs continued attention and staunch support from the executive knowledge leader. As will be detailed in this chapter, ABB noticed that this task is complex and with the exit of the leader who formed the basis of its staunchest support, it floundered.

It is the unquestioned conviction of global management experts that knowledge sharing, leveraging, and the broader management of knowledge are the essence of successful transnational corporations. Corporations such as Hewlett-Packard (HP), McDonalds, and Caterpillar, to name a few, would attest their experiences of knowledge generation and sharing, from locations where one would least anticipate to locations that have traditionally been the source of knowledge for the rest of the world. HP has started using knowledge from their R&D centers in Asia, when it was once simply using their Asian centers as implementers of the knowledge generated in the western world. The same is the case with Intel. McDonalds has learned significantly about managing franchise operations from multiple corners of the world and then transferred such learning to their core markets. An increasing number of global corporations are joining the respectable list of companies that are establishing knowledge centers around the world to feed all of their markets. This chapter focuses on a unique attempt in integrating and rationalizing operations around the world by focusing on the information and knowledge requirements, creating organizational structures and processes along the way, to harness the knowledge of the hundreds of organizational sub-units spread around the world. Percy Barnevik specifically tried to generate, share, and leverage knowledge by utilizing job rotation, creating multinational teams of leaders, and by providing the organizational structure to support the overall efforts.

ABB: A BRIEF HISTORY

ABB is a young company, forged through the merger of two sleeping giants of Europe, the first of which is Asea, created in 1890, that has been a flagship of Swedish industry. The second sleeping giant is Brown Boveri of Switzerland, established in 1891 with a towering industrial status in its domestic market. The merged ABB is headquartered in Zurich and was established in 1987, when Percy Barnevik who was the managing director of Asea announced the merger with Brown Boveri to create a potent new force in the global market for electrical systems and equipment. ABB is still one of the leaders in the electrical systems and equipment market in the world despite all their ups and downs. It is to Percy Barnevik's credit that his grand vision of the truly global yet local corporation was realized and established itself firmly in the global markets. Succeeding CEOs have led the company in different directions and attempted to manage the establishment created by Barnevik, with only limited success, and some huge upheavals. Some of the downswings of ABB can be attributed to the abandoning of the matrix organizational structure by later CEOs, arguing that the management of this structure was one of high complexity.

The creation of ABB, initially only a metaphor for the changing economic map of Europe, thanks to Barnevik's knowledge leadership, eventually became more than a metaphor and resulted in triggering a wholesale restructuring of the continent's electrical power industry. With the creation of ABB, Percy Barnevik put in motion a long process of acquisition, restructuring, and growth. In 1989, ABB acquired Westinghouse's transmission and distribution operation involving 25 factories and businesses with $1 billion in revenues. Later that year, Barnevik spent US$1.6 billion to acquire Combustion Engineering, the manufacturer of power-generation and process-automation equipment, a decision that would later backfire and lead to some upheavals resulting from asbestos scandals and lawsuits, creating the need to set aside huge amounts of money as reserve for paying out settlements. Arguably, anticipating the asbestos crisis at the time of the merger would have been very difficult. Estimating the actual damages that the company would incur as a result of lawsuits, though clear in hindsight, would have been even more difficult. The scale of this difficulty would have been bigger than managing the huge global operations. Barnevik initiated and implemented many other acquisitions and the resulting integration efforts which resulted in ABB's 1994 revenues of US$29.4 billions and created a more then mere presence in global markets, with product development, manufacturing, and marketing bases in Europe, the Americas, and Asia. Barnevik's concept of the truly global corporation preceded notions of being a good corporate citizen in Host Country Markets that were to become fashionable much later. In his words, "What I mean by true globalization is not only that you meet global competitors—that you export to other markets and compete with people there—but also that you have a presence in [product] development and, indeed, in manufacturing in many markets" (Taylor 1991).

At its peak, ABB employed 240,000 people around the world and was well balanced on both sides of the Atlantic, with Europe contributing more than 60 percent of its total revenues. Within Europe, its business was split equally between the European Community (EC) and non-EC Scandinavian countries. Barnevik described his company as one with no geographic center, no national axe to grind, and as one that is not homeless, but with many homes. Germany, ABB's largest national market in 1991, contributed 15 percent of total revenues, with North America generating US$7 billion. 15 percent of its revenues in 1991 came from Asia, with over 10,000 employees in India. Another 10,000 were employed in South America by ABB, which was also considered to be one of the most active investors in Eastern Europe. Barnevik was deeply concerned about the severe economic and industrial disintegration of several former Soviet Union republics. In 2004, ABB had US$14.1 billion in earnings with a healthy yet modest profit of US$188 million, well on its way to meeting targets, after its near collapse in 2002. The collapse was triggered by excessive diversification into non-core activities such as re-insurance and credit risk among other businesses, much of which were brought on by later CEOs, with Percy Barnevik out of the picture. The one mistake that can be clearly attributed to Percy Barnevik was the acquisition of Combustion Engineering which left ABB exposed to the massive asbestos liabilities. As argued earlier, this probably could not have been anticipated in its entirety at the time of the acquisition, when the world was not aware of asbestos problems as it is so well aware of today. The fact that ABB's current strength in its revival efforts is centered on its core businesses in power and automation technologies, as it was at its peak in 1991, lends credence to the arguments in favor of Percy Barnevik's efforts at wakening the two sleeping giants in Europe. Percy Barnevik has been ruthlessly crucified in the media, which conveniently missed the fact that the revival is based on a divestment of the businesses that were all brought on board by later CEOs, which Percy Barnevik had nothing to do with in his leadership position. Percy Barnevik got very angry at accusations that his strategies helped run the company down. "I refuse to accept that we were trigger-happy with acquisitions", he said, and argued that the management structure he created was the right way to organize a growing global business. Being made the scapegoat, he said, "has not been much fun" (Bilefsky and Raghavan 2003). Operating in more than 100 countries, ABB is still a leading maker of power-transmission and distribution equipment, such as transformers and circuit breakers, and industrial robots.

GLOBAL KNOWLEDGE MANAGEMENT AT ABB

Industry Week once characterized Percy Barnevik as a person with a prodigious source of personal energy, a boundless grasp of business operations, and a clear determination to enhance his company's competitive mark in industry (McClenahen 1994). *Fortune* characterized Barnevik, a Swede with a Stanford MBA, as one of Europe's tough new managers, who successfully forged a competitive powerhouse out of ABB by taking the concept of leanness to extremes (Hofheinz 1993). Barnevik was widely hailed in the world media for having created an organization that was a model of global management of businesses. Barnevik has explained in detail, in many media interviews, his beliefs, practices he instituted, and his overall approach to managing a "multidomestic" enterprise, which by some accounts had become a model for the post-transnational corporation (Agres 1991). Barnevik created a federation of national companies with a global coordination center, spanning so many countries that it seemed stateless, yet entrenched in each of those countries that it seems multidomestic. ABB's and Barnevik's secret to creating such a global powerhouse lies in his seemingly paradoxical management approach: global yet local, centralized yet radically decentralized, big and small. Speaking of the organizational structure that backs this approach, Barnevik said:

> That's where the matrix comes in. The matrix is the framework through which we organize our activities. It allows us to optimize our businesses globally and maximize performance in every country in which we operate. Some people resist it. They say the matrix is too rigid, too simplistic. But what choice do you have? To say you don't like a matrix is like saying you don't like factories or you don't like breathing. It's a fact of life. If you deny the formal, you wind up with an informal one—one that's much harder to reckon with. As we learn to master the matrix, we get a truly multidomestic organization. (Taylor 1991)

The resistance that Barnevik alludes to in this quote has clear links to his successors not paying enough attention to the matrix structure, which was the single most important reason for ABB's collapse after Barnevik's exit from the CEO position. Not managing the matrix by giving attention to the intricate details was responsible for ABB's poor performance after it reached its peak, compounded by excessive diversification into non-core activities such as reinsurance and credit businesses. Thus, the responsibility for ABB's collapse should rest squarely on the shoulders of Barnevik's successors, rather than attempting to make a scapegoat out of him. Other instances in global business attest to the veracity of this assertion. Matsushita, the owners of the powerful Panasonic brand were for a long time organized as either a matrix structure or a product team structure, a variant of the matrix structure. Phillips, its onetime major competitor had a long struggle with managing its own matrix structure, with a string of rapidly succeeding CEOs unable to harness this structure in its pure form or in its informal version. Directly linked to this incapability is the fact of high CEO turnover at Phillips, in comparison to Matsushita's fairly stable top executive leadership. The end result of this situation is the well-known superiority of Matsushita in the global electronics business, triumphing over a not so feeble competitor in Phillips. As pointed out at the beginning of this chapter, the context of global business is very complex, thereby calling for complex solutions. Companies that are willing and able to take on this complexity, such as Matsushita or ABB for the duration of Barnevik's executive leadership, are much more capable of coming up with the trumps needed for sustainable success. The moment Barnevik was out of the picture at ABB, his successors mismanaged the matrix and triggered the collapse.

THE MATRIX KNOWLEDGE NETWORK

Percy Barnevik created an organizational structure that covers the world with a matrix that by its description reveals the level of complexity. The overarching objective of the matrix structure is to facilitate rapid movement of information and knowledge across locations and to enable quick decision-making by executives at all levels. Barnevik's creation is a clear illustration of executive knowledge leadership in action. The matrix embraces 5000 profit centers and 1300 separate companies. The structure enables the company to be global and local, big and small, decentralized with some level of centralized control. At the time of its creation, the matrix spanned 51 business areas each headed by a manager, and 41 countries, each headed by a country manager. A representation of the matrix implemented by Barnevik is shown in Figure 9.1.

It is well known that the matrix structure is the best suited organizational form to combine optimal levels of centralization and decentralization, thereby enabling the quick movement of information and knowledge across the horizontal dimension of the structure and from top to bottom of the vertical layers of the structure. The matrix in ABB consists of the horizontal layers of business areas such as power transformers, locomotives, automation

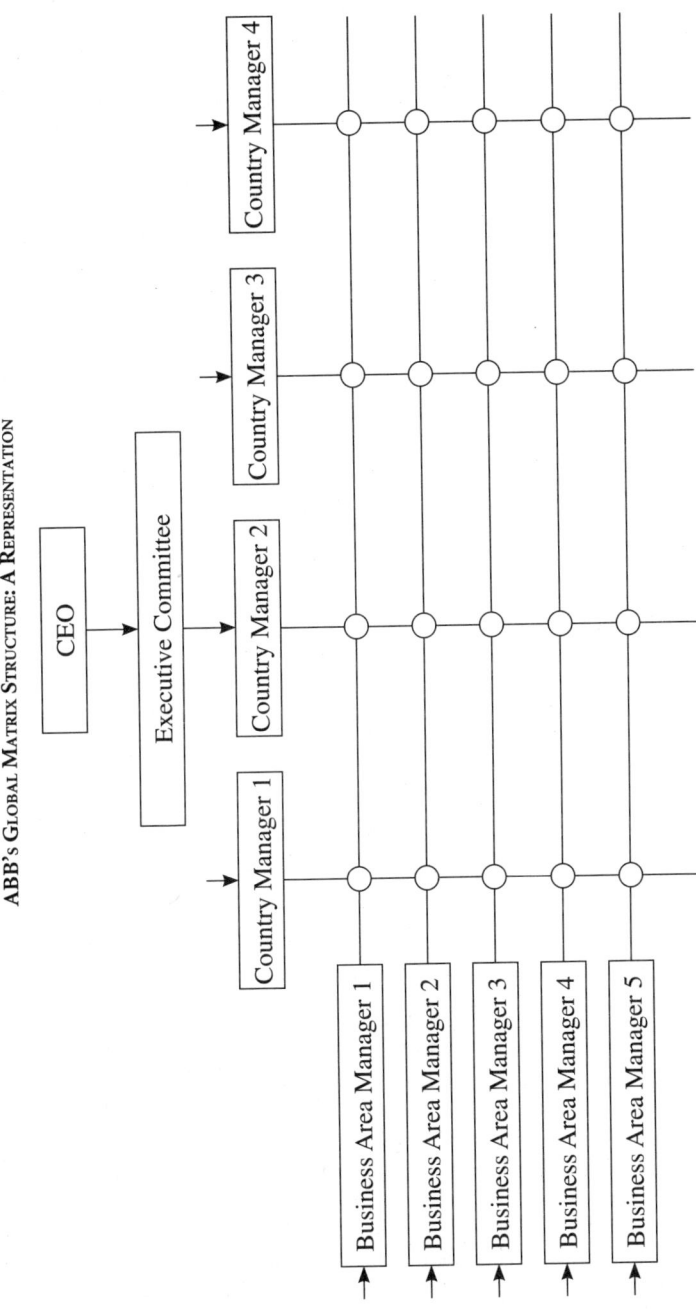

Figure 9.1
ABB's Global Matrix Structure: A Representation

equipment, etc. The verticals in the ABB's structure consist of each of the countries that it is located in. To effectively manage a matrix structure, which is complex by definition and core constitution, Percy Barnevik created an executive committee consisting of 13 of ABB's top managers, each of whom also had responsibility for a business segment. This executive committee structure at the top was necessary, according to him, to facilitate quick decision-making and careful monitoring of the developments around the world. The matrix actually works when these busy executives meet every three weeks for a whole day, sitting together and discussing their collective responsibilities for the global strategy and performance of the company. Decisions made in this executive committee are directly and quickly communicated to their direct reports who are the business area managers and the country managers, to put the implementation process under way.

Percy Barnevik visualized and implemented transparency through a management information system called Abacus, which collected monthly performance data on their 5000 profit centers and compared performance with budgets and forecasts. Thus, Barnevik's knowledge leadership utilized the technological network to aid and complement the socio-cognitive network of the teams of executives. The MIS allowed ABB to aggregate and disaggregate results by business segments, countries, and companies within countries. The executive committee is charged with the specific responsibility of looking for early signs of businesses becoming more or less healthy by examining several parameters, such as new orders, invoicing, margins, cash flows, and looking for trends in these and other areas. Responding to a question on information necessary for fast decision-making Barnevik said:

> Let's say the industry is behind budget. I look to see which of the five BAs in the segment are behind. I see that process automation is way off. So I look by country and learn that the problem is in the United States and that it's poor margins, not weak revenues. So the answer is obvious—a price war has broken out. That doesn't mean I start giving orders. But I want to have informed dialogues with the appropriate executives. (Taylor 1991)

This executive committee, backed by Abacus (MIS), is the combination of technological and non-technological knowledge networks that provide the much needed rationalization of operations across the multiple countries and business areas to enhance achievement of organizational objectives.

The business area managers (BA managers), the country managers, and the presidents of the local companies report to this executive committee. Barnevik stressed that these managers must understand their roles and appreciate that they are complementing each other and not competing. It is the executive committee's responsibility to ensure that this spirit of complementarity pervades the matrix. Barnevik put in a lot of thought into defining the roles of each of these managers to ensure that they complement each other rather than compete with each other. Describing the role of the business area managers, Barnevik said, "The BA managers are crucial people. They need a strong hand in crafting strategy, evaluating performance around the world, and working with the teams made up of different nationalities" (Taylor 1991). In addition to the responsibilities and authority implied in the description, Barnevik also ensured that there was enough autonomy for each of the presidents of the local companies within which these businesses existed. In this context he said:

> BA managers don't own the people working in any business area around the world. They can't order the President of a local company to fire someone or to use a particular strategy in union negotiations. On the other hand, they can't let their role degrade into a statistical coordinator or scorekeeper. (Taylor 1991)

Barnevik expected his business area managers to handle this difficult balancing act, which according to him would exist regardless of the presence or absence of the matrix, only at a more informal level.

The role of country managers was visualized differently in the overall scheme of the matrix. Barnevik saw them as regional line managers, the equivalent of the CEO of a local company, with sufficient respect for ABB's global objectives. The BA managers' presence and hence the presence of the matrix is to ensure that ABB's global objectives are respected and honored. In his words:

> The President of, say, ABB Portugal can't tell the BA manager for low voltage switchgear or drives to stay out of his hair. He has to cooperate with the BA managers to evaluate and improve what's happening in Portugal in those businesses. He should be able to tell a BA manager, "You may think the plant in Portugal is up to standards, but you're being too loose". Turnover and absenteeism is twice the Portuguese average. There are problems with the union and it's the managers' fault. (Taylor 1991)

While the BA managers and the country managers have to work in cooperation with each other and the presidents of the local companies, under the guidance of the executive committee, the presidents of the local companies had a slightly different role. In addition to being excellent profit center managers, they also had to be answerable to two bosses effectively. In Barnevik's words, "After all they have two sets of responsibilities. They have a global boss, the BA manager who creates the rules of the game by which they run their businesses. They also have their country boss, to whom they report in a local setting" (Taylor 1991). The country managers, of course, help in the coordination with the BA managers and the global business objectives of ABB. Barnevik expected the presidents of the local companies to have the self-confidence to handle the ambiguity, not be paralyzed by it, even if they receive conflicting signals, and to possess the integrity not to play one boss against the other. Thus, the matrix implemented by Percy Barnevik was well thought out and designed with careful role descriptions and appropriate matching of responsibility and authority required to run the businesses smoothly. Barnevik did agree that as with most activities in global business, all this was much easier said than done. The fact that ABB achieved much of its growth through acquisitions and restructuring made the task a little more complex than most other situations. The country managers of the acquired businesses, who were once heading national strongholds had to be convinced of the benefits of being part of the federation of companies. Under Barnevik's guidance, carefully chosen executives from the executive committee and outside of it went to these different companies and obtained their support and cooperation.

Barnevik gave the example of Finland, where they were able to obtain success in soliciting such cooperation, among the many other success stories. ABB acquired Stromberg, a Finnish power and electrical products company, in 1986. By virtue of having access to worldwide distribution, being part of ABB Stromberg agreed to scale down the product range drastically to allow for other ABB companies to focus on their strengths and for Stromberg to focus more strongly on its strengths. It became a recognized world leader in Drives as a result of this merger, rather than being a so-so player in the entire product range it used to produce before the federation. ABB Stromberg had become one of the most profitable companies in the entire group, with a return on capital of 30 percent, and increased its exports to Germany and France by about 10 times. Thus, as in any network, a system of mutual incentives and contributions was used to seek and obtain willing cooperation and support of the constituent units. Barnevik's main objective was to ensure that they gain more monetarily when they lose some autonomy. This was at the core of the success achieved in this global (transnational) coordination effort. None of this would be possible without the socio-cognitive knowledge (and information) network provided by the matrix, in combination with the technological network of information.

THE MATRIX: A VIEW FROM THE GROUND UP

To put things in perspective, let us look at the matrix from the ground level, from the point of view of one business area manager. ABB is the world's leading manufacturer of power transformers, expensive products used in the transmission of electricity over long distances, with annual revenues in the early 1990s of well over US$1 billion. In an industry that is characterized by moderate growth and intense price competition, ABB's power transformer business achieved remarkable performance with its consistent and increasing profitability. Its revenues are nearly four times that of its nearest competitor. The BA manager for power transformers is located in Mannheim, Germany, overseeing a global business with 25 factories in 16 countries. He has a small team of mixed nationalities to help guide him in this effort. Drawing from this multi-nationality pool of managers, the BA manager makes decisions on strategy and global optimization, and monitors the trajectory of his business. This team of managers considers information and knowledge of each of the local markets in deciding which factories are going to produce what products, what export markets they will serve, how the factories should pool their expertise and knowledge, including research funds for the benefit of the business worldwide. Incidentally, ABB has become a prototype for global R&D management by coordinating a US$1.9 billion R&D budget among 1300 electrotechnical companies (Agres 1991). The matrix also facilitated the BA manager to search for, track, and rationalize talent around the world. In Barnevik's words, "He also tracks talent—the 60 or 70 real standouts around the world. Say we need a plant manager for a new company in Thailand. The BA head should know of three or four people who could help in Thailand" (McClenahen 1994).

In explaining the view of the matrix from the ground up, we can at this point think that it is possible to leave the organization as described without regard to ABB's mix of business areas in multiple countries. In fact this was the approach used by Phillips in the example cited earlier, which lost out to Matsushita in the Global electronics market as a result of Matsushita's efforts at not being satisfied with simply optimizing business areas with managers responsible for their global coordination. Matsushita, like ABB, went further and brought in the other dimension of the countries and their managers, in more or less similar terms, to complete the matrix. Barnevik used the example of the power transformer company in Norway that employs 400 people. ABB Norway's business did not end with power transformers and employed 10,000 other people in the country. Thus the benefits for the BA manager for power transformers and thus the benefit for ABB on the whole are much higher. This is because the coordination of Norway's power transformer operations with its other (larger) operations in power generation, switchgear, and process automation are critical. That brings in the country managers, ABB Norway in this instance, with headquarters in Oslo. ABB Norway, as in the case of other countries where ABB has operations, is headed by a CEO, to ensure that ABB Norway operates as a Norwegian company rather than as an multinational company. The fundamental reason for this approach is to truly create a trans-national corporation in image, behavior, and attitude. There are many countries around the world, and ABB is currently in 100 of them, where the government would not trust some faraway foreign company. Thus the opportunities for synergy were very clear to the visionary Barnevik right from the beginning when he initiated the Asea and Brown Boveri merger. He simply demonstrated knowledge leadership in utilizing the matrix to lead the company from one of pillar of strength to another. His effective leadership of ABB since 1987 led to such a tremendous growth in revenues, profits, and new orders (critical in this business) that in 1992 he won the Silver Award for *Financial World*'s CEO of the year. As a result of his achievement in creating ABB as a global powerhouse in electrical equipment that is bigger than Westinghouse and could go head to head with GE, he was consulted by International Business Machine Corporation (IBM) to help reduce its overstaffed bureaucracy, in addition to being put on DuPont's board of directors. In addition to efforts outlined here in terms of his knowledge leadership, Barnevik also had to do other things to make his giant dance, including cutting one in five jobs, closing dozens of factories, and drastically reducing the headquarter's strength. He created a corps of about 250 managers to manage more than 200,000 employees.

Barnevik's knowledge leadership also manifested itself in terms of what has been referred as supplier-focused knowledge management, as discussed in Chapter 6. ABB supplied its 5,000 profit centers by centralizing its purchase at Mannheim, Germany, run by two Swedes, who reported at board meetings on how much they saved each time. In addition to focusing on cost savings, to complement their international R&D management, ABB involved suppliers in their product design and reaped much more in benefits than costs. Early supplier involvement in product design is a characteristic feature of supplier-focused knowledge management, as described earlier. Instead of giving the suppliers a new design, the company asks it to create its own design to optimize on costs. Anderson, one of the Swedes who runs the global purchasing center said:

> One Japanese supplier was asked to take on such a project. The result was a new part 30% cheaper than the earlier version. Our first reaction was to get angry and ask why they did not do this before. The answer was, "you didn't ask". (Hofheinz 1993)

ABB is developing a family of suppliers for each of its businesses, like a Japanese Keiretsu. By coordinating global purchasing from a central location, they can pick from anywhere in the world rather than just local suppliers preferred by Keiretsus. Barnevik explained his logic in this context as follows, "If you have ten suppliers for porcelain for your transformers and you are by far the biggest transformer maker in the world, you can cut those ten down to three." The resulting supplier network can provide high quality, short delivery times, and high speed to market for ABB.

> Any idiot can reduce a price by 10% to become more competitive, Barnevik said, but if you can offer an electric power transmission cable under the Baltic one year earlier than your competitor can, that is of tremendous value to the customer, and your competitor can't touch you. First you have to shrink your own business, then your supplier network. (Hofheinz 1993)

ABB's global search for suppliers sometimes takes them into countries that other companies that are not so transnationally minded might avoid. In addition to being able to source from those markets, ABB also ensures that their presence in those markets, creating jobs and export bases, also gets them businesses in those countries. Thus, Barnevik's knowledge leadership extends beyond organizational structure into the realm of supply chain, not to mention politics in the various governments around the world, and other domains that affect ABB.

Political and Other Challenges

Although Europeans admired Percy Barnevik, they thought he was a tough slavemaster. Barnevik also did not make many friends, except among investors, in his quest to make ABB leaner, meaner, and more effective. ABB Germany is a case in point. Brown Boveri had operated in Germany for a long time, operating under the German system of codetermination and work councils having significant impact on operations. Codetermination was a fact of life in Switzerland as well. This created a setting, which made it difficult for Barnevik to implement his rationalization plans at a location which was a technology driven, low profit organization, and an underperformer. The German operation was big with an employee base of 35,000. When ABB announced its plans of reducing the workforce by 10 percent (about 4,000 employees), there was a huge uproar. The executives sent in to handle the situation were faced with strikes, demonstrations, and barricades. Much of this resistance was said to have been fed by local management. When the unions realized the complete nature of the plans and realized its importance, thanks to ABB executives, they came on board and dropped all resistance. Three years from the merger, ABB Germany had grown to three times its size in 1987 and experienced continuously increasing profits. Barnevik says that one of the lessons learnt from the German experience is that one has to be factual, quick, and neutral. Moving boldly, avoiding delay in decision-making through prolonged investigations, is more valuable than can be realized. Barnevik said:

> A long series of small changes just prolongs the pain. Finally, you have to accept a fair share of mistakes. I tell my people that if we make 100 decisions and 70 of them turn out to be right, that's good enough. I'd rather be roughly right and fast than exactly right and slow. Because the costs of delay are

vastly greater than the costs of an occasional mistake. I won't deny that it was absolutely crazy around here for the first few months after the merger. We had to get the matrix in place—we couldn't debate it—and we had to figure out which plants to close and which would stay open. We took ten of our best people, the superstars, and gave them six weeks to design the restructuring. We called it the Manhattan project. I personally interviewed 400 people, virtually day and night, to help select and motivate people to run our local companies. (Taylor 1991)

Benefits of the Matrix

The matrix at ABB makes it easier for the organization to leverage technology around the world. Global coordination of R&D is a significant gainer of the matrix system. It makes it easier for executives such as Gerhard Schulmeyer, a German who headed the automation business as well as the US businesses, to make use of technology from other countries. He relied on European technology to convert a nuclear reactor in Michigan to a natural gas-fired plant. He said that technology from Switzerland is much better than that available in the US for servicing steam turbines. With the matrix, executives are aware of what technologies are available where. In addition, other executives are aware of how other units are performing, as a result of the high-levels of interaction and integration allowed for by the matrix. If one factory is lagging, solutions to common problems can be discussed and worked out across borders. Barnevik says that it might be better to focus on the synergies from collaboration rather than the conflicts that have to be handled in the matrix.

Barnevik anticipated the growth in cross-border mergers within Europe as a result of the EC and elsewhere as well. He realized that this growth in cross-border mergers was going to demand higher levels of productivity, efficiency, and profitability from any corporation. He envisioned an approach based on this knowledge, and put in a piece of organizational technology, namely, the matrix, and toiled day and night to realize his vision. Envisioning is a process of rigorous data collection and analysis as some leadership experts have suggested. Thus envisioning, at least of the variety displayed by Barnevik, is based on knowledge and information. The amazing growth and the powerful global presence that ABB achieved were due to his knowledge leadership. It is unfortunate that his successors have not built on the platform that he created and stabilized, and have actually let it slide, at least temporarily.

10

KNOWLEDGE MANAGEMENT IN RETAIL

LI & FUNG

*Finding the best suppliers (for a Western Retailer) at any given time takes enormous research—so much, indeed, that companies are increasingly deciding that it no longer pays to do it in-house. Instead they outsource the **knowledge-gathering to Li & Fung**, which has an army of 3600 staff roaming 37 countries ("a machete in one hand, a laptop in the other," as Victor Fung likes to caricature them) for the purpose.*

There are indeed companies in Asia that have based their entire business model on introducing buyers to suppliers via the web—Alibaba in China and Global Sources in Hong Kong are the best-known. But none matches the growth of Li & Fung. It uses the internet to make supply chains more transparent, but it never confuses the internet with knowledge. Its real value lies in its power to influence factory owners, leaning on them to reserve capacity, monitoring quality, and so forth.

—The Economist 2001

If globalization is the biggest phenomenon to affect businesses and their leaders in a long time, the growth of organized retailing around the globe is a subset of this macro phenomenon. All the big industrial houses of India are gearing up to get into this huge sector of retailing to obtain the highest return on capital for their investors. In addition to the high returns on investment, these huge industrial houses are also aiming to secure a strong presence in the retailing sector to facilitate the distribution of their own products through these retail chains while simultaneously trying to ensure that their brand-building efforts are not offset by greater brand-building by competitors who are able to get there first. Establishing chains of retail outlets across vast countries, not to mention across continents and broader regions of the world, is a formidable task and places a huge information and knowledge load on the business leaders. Some multinational companies based in Asia have conquered this challenge of huge information and knowledge loads and successfully established highly integrated supply chains from manufacturing to retail. Li & Fung of Hong Kong is one of these rare companies, whose presence extends from trading to distribution and logistics, to retailing. They are engaged in each of these different sub-sectors to provide highest value to their clients. Electronic Data Interchanges (EDI) between traditional retailers such as Levi Strauss & Co. and their multiple suppliers have been fairly common in this sector for ages. These EDIs help the retailers in conveying information in real-time to their suppliers and keeping them abreast of market trends, sales patterns, and therefore requirements for new orders. Knowledge leadership in retails pushes this envelope further by creating a concept that takes such real-time information movement to its extreme and establishing a virtual and real network of manufacturers, subcontractors, and logistics providers, spanning the entire value-chain. Victor Fung and his associates at Li & Fung exhibit such knowledge leadership by creating an integrated solutions provider in the retail context in the global arena. This chapter will focus on the knowledge leadership exhibited by this pioneer company in global markets.

Wealth does not pass beyond the third generation. Li & Fung, one of the oldest trading houses in Hong Kong, and its family owners were facing the fear and threat implied by this Chinese saying. This saying could very well have come true had it not been for a phone call in 1972 from the mother of William Fung and his older brother Victor Fung. Both men who were educated in US universities, with one of them teaching at Harvard University, were told, "If one of you boys doesn't come back and help your father, he's going to kill himself working hard." William, a computer science graduate from Princeton returned that same year and Victor followed two years later. Li & Fung, a multinational group of companies, was founded in Guangzhou, the People's Republic of China (PRC), in 1906. The Li & Fung group, with 2006 revenues of US$10.4 billion, employing 25,000 people in 40 countries across the world is driving strong growth in trading (export sourcing), retailing, and distribution services. Li & Fung Ltd, the export-trading arm of the group, is one of the largest multinational export trading houses, with locations in close to 40 countries around the world. The group engages in retailing through Convenience Retail Asia (CRA), a publicly listed company, operating three retailing businesses: Circle K, Toys "R" Us, and Branded Lifestyle, with the store network extending from Greater China to South Korea, Thailand, Malaysia, Singapore, Indonesia, and the Philippines. The Integrated Distribution Services group (IDS) runs the distribution arm of the group by providing corporate clients with services in three core business areas: marketing, logistics, and manufacturing. Although all three businesses of the group are driving strong growth, this was seriously threatened in the late 1990s with the advent of the internet. The threat of disintermediation, that the internet would allow companies to buy all their parts and components online from and through giant electronic marketplaces, was an ever-present danger (Holstein 2002). But this was based on a mistaken assumption and confusing the internet for knowledge, which Li & Fung, thanks to the two brothers did not succumb to. William Fung, managing director and CEO of the group says, "We've moved from being the perennial Chinese sort of middleman doing everything you associate with my grandfather's (the founder) days to fully embracing the supply chain management concept" (Holstein 2002).

Victor, a former Harvard professor, and current chairman of the group, and William have instituted their own brand of supplier-focused knowledge management, discussed in an earlier chapter, to turn the organization around from its crisis of the late 1990s. By virtue of its presence in sourcing, retailing, and integrated distribution services, the company combines customer-focused knowledge management with the same on the supply side to provide end-to-end services across the whole value-chain in retail. The company's list of retail clients is simply impressive, to say the least. Rather than being threatened by the internet and other new technologies, the two brothers set out to understand it and harness its potential as it applied to this age-old business which once traded in porcelain, bamboo, rattan ware, and paper-sealed firecrackers, which it is credited with inventing (Magretta 1998). The company established a tradition of innovation in 1907, which has come in handy on multiple occasions, by inventing paper-sealed firecrackers, which were much lighter than the mud-sealed firecrackers resulting in drastically lower import duties and alleviating the dust problems associated with the traditional firecrackers. Today, this tradition of innovation, combined with the knowledge leadership efforts of its leaders, helps in providing innovative alternatives to the traditional agency model of outsourcing for materials and components for the world's major retailers. Instead of simply working as an agent for a fee, Li & Fung provides innovative alternatives to clients including collaborating with them in establishing warehouses in the heart of China (or other countries), thereby not simply being a sourcing solution provider and transporter, but leveraging their complex web of relationships to engage in the actual operations leading to higher market shares and distribution coverage for their clients. Speaking of such an innovative alternative arrangement worked out with Wal-Mart, Mr Fung explained, "We are not being just an agent. We are involved in design, manufacturing and getting into marketing in the US, and delivery to the warehouse of Wal-Mart. It's a different type of margin (Holstein 2002)." The company is jumping up in the supply chain by dealing in information and specializing in the most optimum way to manage information in the whole value-chain.

Before they were faced with trying to understand and harness the internet and related technologies, they were faced with a few other problems and the need to preside over a few other transformations, in the series of transformations that have been brought about at Li & Fung, which is responsible for its strong global position today. In 1988, the two brothers decided that it was time to buy the company from the rest of the family. They underwent the family version of the Management Buyout (MBO), borrowing heavily to finance the deal, and paying over 80 percent premium above market value. In Dr Victor Fung's words, "At that time, with the 1997 handover looming, a lot of family members wanted to migrate from Hong Kong. My brother and I had a lot of faith in the future but other family members thought differently. The family was also getting bigger and bigger. Grandfather had 11 children. I have 35 cousins. A lot of family groups were in this situation. Many ended up in broken factions" (*Business Times Singapore* 2005). Taken private after the buyout, Li & Fung was restructured into two core businesses, namely, export trading and retail, with the integrated distribution services to come later in 1999. The retailing arm grew through joint ventures, franchising, and a combination of listed and unlisted entities. The distribution services were added on through acquisitions. Li & Fung is active in acquisitions even today with its August 2007 acquisition of Peter Black International (PB), the supplier of footwear to Marks & Spencer, and its June 2007 acquisition of C Group, a Hong Kong based international health, beauty, and cosmetics supply chain. The PB group has offices in England, Hong Kong, China, India, and Italy. Thus, through a combination of restructuring and an ongoing process of acquisitions, the two Fung brothers have heralded the company firmly into the era of professional management. Many of the firm's managers are professional managers who are not members of the family, although the two brothers have recently included their children in the management of the company.

Before becoming public again in 1992, the Fung brothers brought in a lot of outside talent, created small entrepreneurial divisions for each of these 'John Waynes' to lead, and combined it with annual planning and profit sharing along with quarterly performance reviews. Many of these management practices were unknown to family-run businesses in the region. They treated each of their division heads like John Wayne type characters by giving them a lot of autonomy, making them responsible for their own profit centers, and offering stock options. In addition, they have also been able to attract top talent by allowing for the potential movement of people all the way to the top of the organization, and not limiting it to only family members, regardless of the shareholding.

KNOWLEDGE LEADERSHIP: TECHNOLOGICAL AND SOCIAL NETWORKS

Having separated business and family and having ensured that the family was happy, the Fung brothers turned their attention to survival and growth in an industry that was facing the threat of disintermediation by the internet. In addition to harnessing and leveraging internet based technologies, Li & Fung began to put their understanding of the value of information and knowledge in the global apparel industry into action. One key aspect of such an understanding was not to confuse the internet with knowledge. This resulted in the massive use of the internet in some parts of the world and reliance on the old fax machine, telephones, and old-fashioned networks of relationships in other parts of the world. Applying all this in the context of the management of the value-chain resulted in highly effective supplier-focused knowledge management and customer-focused knowledge management. Li & Fung set up its first intranet in 1995 and its first extranet in 1997, a fairly early adoption of the technology.

Li & Fung established and maintained an internet-based network of information and knowledge flow with about 75 percent of its customers, and large retailers in the United States including Avon, Coca-Cola, Kohl's and Disney. They have used this network of information flows to move up in the value-chain, similar to how companies moved up in the industrial and consumer electronics industry a decade or so ago, thereby ensuring higher margins and much more aggressive growth. They have been able to double their profits once in three years over the last decade as a result of these efforts. A major licensing deal with Levi Strauss & Co. illustrates this jumping up the value-chain as a result of leveraging knowledge. Under the agreement, Li & Fung would sell its own Levi's brand of tops directly to US retailers, by engaging in the design, manufacturing, and marketing in the US, and rounding it off by directly delivering it to the major retailers directly.

Very few retailers are able to manage their own manufacturing to retain control over the process and to better feel the pulse of changes in trends. An increasing number of retailers are handing this responsibility over to outsourcing companies such as the powerful and fast Li & Fung (Lee-Young and Barnett 2001). Babur Rafiq, who heads Levi's Asian sourcing operations in Singapore, says of Li & Fung, "For certain products, especially seasonal ones, they can do a better, faster job." Located in the center of the garment outsourcing industry, Hong Kong, Li & Fung operates in this business without owning and running factories that make garments, unlike other companies in the business. Instead of owning and running factories, machines, and fabrics, Li & Fung deals only in information, relying on a vast network of more than 7,500 suppliers in 40 countries. William Fung explains, "There are no secrets in the actual manufacturing. I mean a shirt is a shirt. We would rather build on something proprietary, like what information it takes to make that shirt faster or more efficiently" (*Asiaweek* 2000). As an order comes in from, for instance, Levi Strauss, Li & Fung uses personalized websites and e-mail to fine tune specifications with the customer. It then takes those instructions and feeds them into its intranet to find the right supplier of raw materials and the right factory for assembling the clothes. In addition to this the task of designing the garment, actual marketing of it, and subsequent delivery directly to retail store locations, you now have Li & Fung's knowledge solution to the whole process. Some of this work, in some parts of the world, is done without any use of modern technology, but substituted by old-fashioned social networks churning and weaving information. Instead of connecting the thousands of manufacturers who make its products through its extranet systems, Li & Fung chooses to rely on personal visits, phones, faxes, and couriers in countries such as China, the Philippines, Bangladesh, other Asian countries, and Guatemala (Holstein 2002). Li & Fung has another reason for not wanting these locations to be linked through its extranet. To ensure control over the process, it wants its employees to physically ensure that the materials have arrived or progressed to appropriate points in the value-chain process such as production, shipping, etc. The quality of data from these locations could be troublesome to deal with for the company. Although technology is an enabler according to William Fung, it may never connect the entire supply-chain in these locations because of the vagaries of the other infrastructure facilities and more importantly to the lack of well-developed relationships with managers in these locations. In Victor Fung's words:

> At one level, Li & Fung is an information node, flipping information between our 350 customers and our 7500 suppliers. We manage all that today with a lot of phone calls and faxes and on-site visits. That's the guts of the company. Soon we will need a sophisticated information system with very open architecture to ac-commodate different protocols from suppliers and from customers, one robust enough to work in Hong Kong and New York as well as in places like Bangladesh, where you can't always count on a good phone line. (Magretta 1998)

The company's competitive advantage lies in doing something that no computer can do, that is to deconstruct an order and use "distributed manufacturing" to make it. In the case of polo shirts for instance, this means buying American cotton, knitting and dyeing in China because of speed and cost, and sewing in Bangladesh. Such 'distributed manufacturing' optimizes on both costs and speed, not to mention quality in higher-value added processes. Thus, for attaché cases, for instance, Li & Fung buys leather in India, ships it to South Korea for tanning, then to China for final assembly with metal fittings from Japan. Explaining how this reaches into the supply chain and shortens the buying cycle, Victor Fung said:

> Think about what happens when you outsource manufacturing. The easy approach is to place an order for finished goods and let the supplier worry about contracting for the raw materials like fabric and yarn. But a single factory is relatively small and doesn't have as much buying power, that is, it is too small to demand faster deliveries from its suppliers. (Magretta 1998)

For the vast variety of products occupying retail shelves around the world, Li & Fung has information and knowledge on where each step of the value-chain will add value to the process and the final outcome, in addition to the valuable knowledge and skills to execute each of these processes in the best location.

Technological Network

For large customers such as Coca-Cola, Disney, Levi Strauss, the Limited, etc., Li & Fung established dedicated extranet sites, now in its fifth generation of refinement known as XTS 5. XTS is also linked to its own network of offices, where it has 5,000 people supervising the manufacturing of customer items. The nature of the network connections vary based on the technological sophistication of the host country, with more sophisticated data and image transfer capabilities in countries where this is possible. In other locations, they rely more on e-mail and Lotus Notes. Using HP-Compaq computers, Oracle database software, the company has largely designed and written the software that makes up the XTS, which is being offered to more and more of its customers over time. The technological network with manufacturers is another story, however, as explained earlier. What the company does with this technology and Microsoft's *Biztalk* to better connect front-end orders from all customers with its back-end systems is more important in contributing to its edge in the business over others who have tried the all-tech route and failed miserably (Holstein 2002). This technology provides the advantages of speed and flexibility to a business that is facing shorter and shorter inventory cycles, with what used to be products for four seasons now reduced to new products every two weeks. The retail customers can track their orders on the website and make last-minute changes. Whereas five years ago, the company used to deliver on orders in five months, these days, with the new technology, customers can cancel orders online until the material is woven, they can change the color until the fabric is dyed, and they can change the design until the fabric is cut (Lee-Young and Barnett 2001). Having harnessed the internet technologies, Li & Fung is poised for more aggressive growth in parts of the world where its presence is not felt yet.

Social Network

In many parts of the world, however, its core strength in leveraging information and knowledge still rests on the complex web of relationships they have built over time, especially in Asia. In Victor Fung's words:

> We come in and look at the whole supply chain. We know the Limited is going to order 100,000 garments, but we don't know the style or the colours yet. The buyer will tell us that five weeks before delivery. The trust between us and our supply network means that we can reserve undyed yarn from

the yarn supplier. I can lock up capacity at the mills for the weaving and dyeing with the promise that they'll get an order of a specified size, five weeks before delivery. (Magretta 1998)

In addition to the close web of relationships built with the supply network, Li & Fung organizes itself along customer divisions to further enhance their ability to deliver value to each of them. Unlike most companies that say they are customer-focused by designing systems that hopefully fits most of their customers, Li & Fung approach it in a different way.

We organize for the customer. Almost all trading companies with extensive networks of suppliers are organized geographically, with the country units as the profit centers. As a result, it is hard for them to optimize the value-chain. Their country units are competing against one another for business. Our basic operating unit is the division. Whenever possible, we will focus an entire division on serving one customer. We may serve smaller customers through a division structured around a group of customers with similar needs. We have, for example, a theme-store division serving a handful of customers such as Warner Brothers stores and Rainforest Café. This structuring of the organization around customers is very important— remember that what we do is close to creating a customized value chain for every customer order. So customer-focused divisions are the building blocks of our organization. (Magretta 1998)

The contribution of such customer-focused divisions to the management of information and knowledge related to their business is immense and today spans from sourcing, to design, to manufacturing, and to final marketing and delivery. All this is accomplished with their three broad groups operating in trading, retailing, and integrated distribution services.

Just like any other global company with operations dispersed in many countries, Li & Fung also faces its share of the informal matrix problems, alluded to in the previous chapter, between the country operations and the customer operations. Similar to the fights between the geographic side of the organization and the product side of the organizations at ABB, Matsushita, Phillips, and scores of other organizations, Li & Fung's operations are also faced with these issues. Their solution, according to their CEO, is to have primary alignment around customers, with every product group executive also having responsibility for one country, to balance the informal matrix. The fundamental issue is to balance both sets of needs and requirements in one location, for which the matrix is inevitable, formally or informally. Thus Li & Fung, like ABB, is fighting the constant battle of being global yet local, being big and small, being centralized and radically decentralized at the same time. Their customer-focused divisions are small and entrepreneurial, with each run as a separate company by a John Wayne like character, shooting from the hip at bad guys, solving problems and taking ownership for the decisions such as merchandising and coordination of production. These John Waynes have considerable operating autonomy backed by financial incentives. Financial controls and operating procedures are centralized and managed tightly. All cash flow and letters of credit are routed through the central office in Hong Kong, guaranteeing payment before order execution, and characterizing a conservative approach to financial management.

The policy committee of the organization, comprising the top 30 people, constitutes the learning community that holds the geographically disperse organization together on a day-to-day basis. This committee meets once in five to six weeks to share information, exchange ideas about best practices pertaining to ethical sourcing or compliance, inspection of factories, and taking responsibility for implementing decisions in their own units. This is another component of their socio-cognitive network for managing knowledge. In Victor Fung's words:

> As the sources of supply explode, managing information becomes increasingly complex. Of course, we have a lot of hard data about performance and about the work we do with each factory. But what we really want is difficult to pin down, a lot of the most valuable information resides in people's heads. What kind of attitude does the owner have? Do we work well together? How good is their international management? That kind of organizational memory is a lot harder to retain and to share. We see the

capturing of such information as the next frontier. You could look at us as a very sophisticated IT system. (Magretta 1998)

Thus, the Fung brothers' knowledge leadership through both the technological and socio-cognitive routes is one fundamental component of their value generation in the fast paced retail environment.

The leadership provided by the Fung brothers has resulted in the company achieving high levels of growth, more than doubling their profits once in every three years in the last decade. They have also been selected as the best managed company more than once, in addition to being selected as the company with the best corporate governance and the best investor relations. Their brand of knowledge leadership in a business dominated by sourcing from locations where even a telephone connection cannot be taken for granted is truly amazing. Their model of professional management blended with family-values serves as an excellent illustration of knowledge leadership in retail.

11

KNOWLEDGE-BASED PERFORMANCE MANAGEMENT STRATEGIES OF LEADERS

It is the key to being able to identify opportunities that others might not see and to exploit those opportunities rapidly and fully. This means that in order to generate extraordinary value for shareholders, a company has to learn better than its competitors and apply that knowledge throughout its businesses faster and more widely than they do. The way we see it, anyone in the organization who is not directly account-able for making a profit should be involved in creating and distributing knowledge that the company can use to make a profit.

The top management team must stimulate the organization, not control it. Its role is to provide strategic directives, to en-courage learning, and to make sure there are mechanisms for transferring the lessons. The role of leaders at all levels is to demonstrate to people that they are capable of achieving more than they can achieve and that they should never be satisfied with where they are now.

—John Browne, British Petroleum
(In an interview with S.E. Prokesch, *HBR*, 1997)

The dominant psychological (attributional) approach to leadership and management of poor performance focuses on managerial biases that take several forms: self-serving biases, gender biases, biased internal attributions, biased responses to correct performance problems, directed at the employee, and organizationally induced helplessness. If managers continue to be informed by these conventional psychological and interpersonal behavioral models of performance management, thereby being biased, it could result in multiple negative consequences, such as poor performance spirals, learned helplessness, leader-subordinate disagreement and conflict, loss of trust of work group, loss of credibility on the part of the manager, and subordinate dissatisfaction and turnover, all of which make for very ineffective management of poor performance. Such ineffective management of poor performance could result in continued poor performance of employees, the units they belong to, and their entire organizations, in addition to seriously affecting subordinate perceptions of leadership provided by these managers. This may result in their eventual loss of credibility and respect, and they may ultimately lose their managerial positions in organizations. The models of Knowledge Leadership presented in these pages are essential elements of a modern approach to performance management. No longer are the conventional models of performance management adequate or even functional.

This chapter develops and presents a knowledge-based model of performance management, following a critical examination of extant models and a subsequent reformulation. Consistent with a Positive Approach to Leadership (PAL), and using existing theoretical ideas that views leadership as essentially a result of positive perceptions by subordinates and followers, this article builds practical propositions that focus on the process through which managers' attributions lead to their behaviors which create the climate for subordinate performance accomplishment. Viewing leadership as the result of a process of positive perceptions is based on a conceptual distinction between managers and leaders, whereby managers are those who perform the duties of the position they occupy, and leaders are those who are perceived to be leaders to varying degrees by subordinates and others in organizations. Much of the logic and thought in this chapter is based on this conceptual distinction between "managers" and "leaders", while also focusing on positive, functional aspects of leadership, such as building trust, building credibility, and enabling subordinates to perform and contribute to overall organizational performance, using knowledge and causal (attributional) analysis.

Conventional wisdom provides a two stage attributional model of leader responses to poor subordinate performance, by stressing the need for understanding the causes of leader behavior, and their responses to inappropriate behavior of subordinates. Subordinate behavior in general and poor performance events in particular are seen as the stimulus or starting point for the analytical model. Acting as information processing "scientists", leaders then look for informational cues to understand the reasons for the poor performance, to determine the appropriate course of action, apparently in an effort to improve performance. However, this conventional wisdom does not assess the negative consequences of either internal or biased attributions that are an inherent part of the models professed, in the form of lowered self-efficacy, supervisor induced helplessness, subsequent lower performance, perceptions of unfairness, etc. At all managerial levels from first line managers to CEOs of organizations, conventional wisdom has focused on the biases in performance attributions and the impression management attempts of managers seeking to look good in the eyes of others. That all of this is counterproductive and questions their very existence has been overlooked.

Some leadership experts do admit that effective leaders are those who are more accurate in their causal analysis, or perhaps are more successful in avoiding some of the biases. However, such admissions fall short of a focus on leader effectiveness and the attributional processes of leaders that leads to positive subordinate performance.

When leadership is viewed as the result of a process of positive perceptions, it becomes imperative to determine the nature of the attribution process used by leaders that leads them to be effective, in addition to being seen as effective in the minds of subordinates and followers. Such perceptions of leadership can be crucial in getting acceptance and commitment to various decisions made by leaders at various levels in the organization, and enable them to obtain the necessary resources to accomplish high performance objectives.

In this chapter, I present a model based on managerial attributions that lead to higher performance levels, in addition to cognitive knowledge structures that serve the same purpose. The next section provides a discussion of the knowledge-based model developed here and outlines the performance management strategies.

A KNOWLEDGE-BASED MODEL
OF PERFORMANCE MANAGEMENT

The model of performance management developed here focuses on key leadership constructs, such as information processing, manager attributions and their accuracy, clarity of cause-effect beliefs possessed, manager behaviors that follow their attributions, mediating variables, such as uncertainty reduction, subordinate self-efficacy, satisfaction, and motivation, and crucial outcome variables, such as leadership perceptions and subordinate performance. Although similar in concept, attributions and cause-effect beliefs referred to in this model pertain to the past and future, respectively. Attributions refer to causal analysis of (immediate) past performance, whereas cause-effect beliefs pertain to causal analysis of actions and their consequences in the future (of course, based on all past experiences, not just immediate past). These variables are linked in a process model in the manner shown in Figure 11.1. The main insight provided by the model is that managerial knowledge and scientific information processing results in

Figure 11.1

KNOWLEDGE-BASED PERFORMANCE MANAGEMENT STRATEGIES OF LEADERS

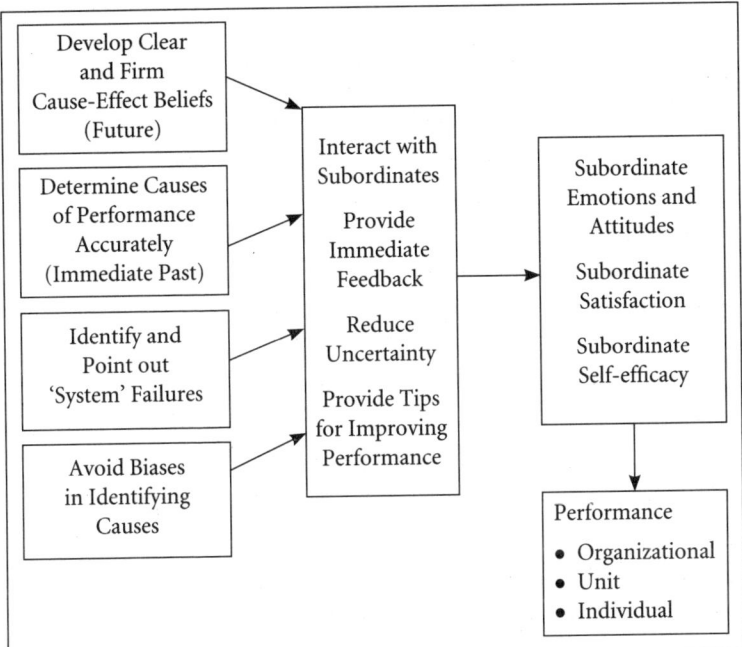

accurate attributions, which then lead to subsequent functional leader interactive behaviors, the nature of the feedback provided, uncertainty reduction, and strategies used to correct performance deficiencies. These behavioral variables are then depicted in terms of their relationship to leader effectiveness through the mediating variables of satisfaction, motivation, and self-efficacy.

Manager Information Processing

It is probably not too surprising to suggest that higher levels of information processing leads to more accurate attributions and avoidance of errors. However, it is not merely a higher dose of information processing that is required, but a careful search of multiple plausible causes. Identification of augmenting and discounting causal schema for each of the multiple plausible causes can lead to more accurate (or reasonable) attributions on the part of managers acting as information processing scientists. Every poor performance episode is likely to have both subordinate dispositional causes and external system causes, at some level of analysis. This is also likely to be true of performance at the organizational level, with both external and internal causes being possible. In any case, it is possible for managers to analyze these multiple plausible causes and arrive at more reasonable (or accurate) attributions. In this context there are two broad approaches to pursue in the determination of accurate attributions, the first using simple schemata (logic) and the second using complex schemata (logic). In more complex instances of poor performance, whether at the individual, unit, or organizational level, it is more fruitful to use complex schemata.

In the case of simple schemata, psychologist Kelley advocated the use of consistency, consensus, and distinctiveness criteria to assess the true nature of the attribution (cause) for the poor performance. Distinctiveness refers to the uniqueness of a behavior in response to a specific task and answers the question of whether or not the subordinate in question performed poorly on all tasks or only on the task in question. Consistency refers to the pattern of behavior over time or across situations by the subordinate, with there being no change in behavior across situations or across time. Consensus refers to the behavior of others and its similarity or lack thereof to the subordinate in question, and answers the question of whether or not many subordinates performed poorly on the task. These three criteria can also be applied while evaluating organizational performance instead of subordinate performance. Attributional accuracy, in this context of simple schemata, is the level of congruence with the antecedent covariation information. Attributions that do not deviate from the logic of the covariation principle using these three criteria are termed veridical or accurate.

However, even Kelley suggested that not all data patterns along the three covariation dimensions lead to clear attributions, because of the simplicity of this schema. Thus, a slightly different approach is needed in complex situations using complex schemata. In the model described here, attributional accuracy, in the context of complex schemata, is defined as the level of congruence with the antecedent discounting and augmenting causal schemata as explained later.

The perceived effect of a particular cause can either be enhanced (augmented) or diminished (discounted) depending upon the consistency of the alternative plausible causes and the observed outcome. In situations of lesser complexity, there are few causes that are consistent with the observed outcome and thus any one cause possesses augmenting schema. In situations of higher complexity, there are multiple causes that are equally consistent with the outcome and thus facilitative of multiple causes. In such a situation, the manager wanting to make more accurate attributions is faced with discounting those causes with less import for the observed outcome, thereby focusing on the cause with the most augmenting schema (or alternatively with the least discounting schema). Attributionally complex individuals, who are known to use such complex schemata, have been found to be more accurate and faster in the judgment of social behaviors, and more accurate in the judgment of attitudes. However, this is true only when elaborate, in-depth processing is also present, thus consistent with the view that both quantity of information and quality of information are related to accuracy of personality judgments. Thus, attributional complexity, combined with higher levels of information processing on the part of leaders can lead to more accurate attributions. Attributional accuracy, thus, has both cognitive and motivational antecedents. This suggests the following strategy:

Performance Management Strategy 1: Select managers high in attributional complexity and train them for in-depth information processing using complex schema.

Manager Attributions

The knowledge-based model of performance management developed here focuses on identifying and examining the strongest qualities of performance managers from two perspectives. First, the predominant perspective is the consideration based on perceptions of leadership by subordinates and followers. Second, the idea that drives this analysis is the explicit focus and consideration of functional and positive attributional behavior of supervisors and managers that lead to effective performance by employees and organizational units. Some leadership experts view leadership as essentially a result of positive perceptions by subordinates and followers. This model focuses on attributions that relate positively to leader effectiveness, including aspects of leadership, such as building trust, building credibility, and enabling subordinates to perform and contribute to overall organizational performance. Biased attributions lead to erosion of trust and credibility as suggested earlier, thereby leading to further poor performance.

Managers who are biased and make inaccurate attributions may not be perceived positively and will be ineffective in correcting performance deficiencies of their subordinates and thus their units. Available evidence that examines subordinate perceptions and reactions to inaccurate and biased attributions does reveal that such attributions are likely to be seen as unfair and result in dissatisfaction among subordinates. Some suggest that self-serving attributional biases are likely to lead to manager-subordinate disagreement, loss of trust in work group, loss of credibility, and subordinate dissatisfaction and turnover. Some others point to more severe consequences of unfavorable and inaccurate attributions of managers on emotional reactions of subordinates leading to downward performance-efficacy spirals. On the contrary, it is functional to make more realistic and more accurate attributions. In laboratory studies, participants made better resource allocation decisions when they were induced to make more accurate attributions than in the inaccurate attribution condition. Such decisions were followed up with behaviors that were functional and in line with the more accurate attributions, all of which resulted in higher levels of performance. Thus, it pays to make more realistic or accurate attributions.

From the perspective of leader effectiveness, the leader-environment-follower interaction theory suggests that the effective leader is one who analyzes the deficiencies in the follower's ability, motivation, role perception, and work environment which inhibit performance, and then takes action to eliminate those deficiencies. A similar type of analysis is essential at the top executive level, as it pertains to poor organizational performance. An accurate analysis of the causes of performance using complex schema is likely to sustain trust of key strategy implementers in the top executive, in addition to enhancing their motivation to implement key strategies. In this attributional context, current knowledge seems to suggest that some kinds of attributions are likely to lead to dysfunctional behaviors and others to functional behaviors that result in strategies for correcting performance deficiencies. Managers have a general reluctance to provide negative feedback, thus avoiding the giving of such feedback, delaying it as much as possible (high feedback latency), and distorting it when further delay is not possible, all in an effort to avoid some of the unpleasant and negative consequences of such feedback. Internal attributions directed towards subordinates, or biased attributions, may be a factor that causes this delay in feedback (latency), distortion of feedback, and more importantly the negative interactive behaviors with subordinates in poor per-formance contexts. However, it is not evident that delaying or distorting feedback does any good for the subordinates. On the contrary, it may enhance apprehension and increase subordinate uncertainty, a condition that is the exact opposite of that which leaders would create.

Attributionally complex individuals engaging in in-depth pro-cessing of information may arrive at more accurate attributions, identifying complex internal causes and complex external causes along the way. Such assessments provide these individuals with more information and more confidence in their information, thereby minimizing the possibility of withdrawal behaviors and feedback latency. Available evidence suggests that accurate attributions lead to positive interactive behaviors, positive interpretation of subordinate behaviors, and most important, the formulation and implementation of integrative strategies to correct performance deficiencies. Thus, accurate attributions results in positive interactive behaviors, leads to lower feedback latencies, and thus results in an environment of low uncertainty for subordinates, all of which is likely to enhance subordinate affect and attitudes positively. Considering all of this in the context of the argument that effective leaders are those who are likely to be accurate in their causal attributions and likely to avoid biased attributions, the following performance management strategy is suggested.

Performance Management Strategy 2: Train managers to be more accurate in their causal analysis and to engage in higher and more positive levels of interactive behaviors.

Corollary 1: Managers who have higher attributional accuracy also have low feedback latencies, which is crucial for leading their units to higher effectiveness.

Corollary 2: Managers who have higher attributional accuracy also have better performance correction strategies, crucial for leading their units to higher effectiveness.

Cause-effect belief knowledge

Manager's knowledge in the form of cause-effect beliefs is an important variable in the context of performance management. Leadership experts have emphasized the importance of cause-effect beliefs knowledge on the part of executive leaders in effective decision-making leading to organizational performance. The work of James McGregor Burns is commonly associated with the field of "transformational leadership." While addressing the topic of leadership and decision-making, Burns emphasized the crucial importance of leaders' understanding of future decisions (based on the past and other knowledge) and their consequences for achieving organizational objectives. Because there is a lot of complexity surrounding executive decision-making, it is very important for decision makers to perform calculations on how to use and adapt chains of cause and effect relevant to their goals. Executive leaders must anticipate how various groups and publics, including subordinates in this context, will react to different decisions and modify their own actions accordingly. What is very important in this context is an understanding on the part of leaders of past decisions and their consequences and anticipation of future decisions and their consequences. Thus leaders need to possess knowledge in the form of cause-effect beliefs and they need to learn from both the past and the present in the continuous formation and refining of their "implicit theories." Such knowledge in the form of cause-effect beliefs is likely to guide these leaders in the choice of the appropriate interactive behaviors to use vis-à-vis subordinates, especially in poor performance contexts. This leads to the following practical conclusion.

Performance Management Strategy 3: Train managers to verbalize and document their knowledge in the form of clear cause-effect beliefs (because these are not always in the conscious realm). This surfaces tacit knowledge and converts it to explicit knowledge, which provides crucial inputs for their positive interactive behaviors vis-à-vis their subordinates, thereby leading their organizations to higher effectiveness.

In addition to the effect of knowledge in the form of cause-effect beliefs on leader interactive behaviors, such knowledge is also important for better development of performance correction strategies by managers. This is consistent with the trait approach to leadership that emphasizes the importance of knowledge as an important leader attribute. While attributions for poor performance are likely to be highly specific to such contexts, knowledge in the form of cause-effect beliefs is likely to be broader and general to the whole work context, regardless of the level of performance. Thus, managers' knowledge in the form of clear and complete cause-effect beliefs are positively related to the development of performance correction strategies by these managers.

> **Corollary:** Managers that have higher levels of knowledge in the form of clear cause-effect beliefs develop better performance correction strategies than others, thereby leading their units to higher effectiveness.

Non-susceptibility to attributional biases

A focus on non-susceptibility to attribution biases by way of conceptualizing and operationalizing such non-susceptibility is more positive than the focus on susceptibility to attributional biases. Attributional complexity and the associated processing of information along the lines of complex schemata, on the part of managers is likely to be one of the key determinants of the degree to which managers are non-susceptible to counterproductive gender, racial, and self-serving attributional biases. The conventional attribution model and a number of subsequent tests of the model focus on gender, racial, and self-serving biases of managerial attributions of poor subordinate performance. As suggested earlier, all of these biases are likely to lead to heightened interpersonal conflict and disrupt the processes of communication between managers and their subordinates affected by all of these biases. These ideas suggest that to be effective, managers need to avoid all kinds of biases, such as gender, racial, and self-serving biases, especially in the context of performance attributions. Much like the performance-efficacy spirals discussed earlier, these biases can lead to attribution-conflict spirals, whereby biased attributions can lead to more severe conflict, which can in turn affect the attributions made in conflict contexts and the choice and interpretation of communication strategies. Moreover, gender and racial biases can also lead to a loss of trust, dissatisfaction, and turnover. Loss of trust can result in the erosion of leadership in the worst case or severely negative perceptions of leadership in the best case scenario. Focusing on the degree to which managers are non-susceptible to such attributional biases may provide a more positive and utilitarian perspective. Therefore, one can conclude that managers who avoid gender and racial biases in attributions of performance are more likely to be effective and perceived more as leaders. The next performance strategy is as follows.

Performance Management Strategy 4: Training managers to be non-susceptible to attribution biases (gender and racial) leads them to develop better performance correction strategies.

Corollary: Training managers to be non-susceptible to attribution biases (gender and racial) leads directly to subordinate satisfaction, thereby resulting in higher perceptions of leadership.

Manager attributions at the unit level

The preceding discussion has highlighted the importance of the accuracy of causal analysis and attributions made by managers and their degree of susceptibility to various biases, both in terms of their effectiveness and leadership perceptions. The analysis so far has focused on the performance of individuals. However, a slightly broader level of analysis at the unit level is also needed for better formulation of a performance management model. Since unit managers are held accountable for the unit's performance, poorly performing units are immediately brought to the notice of those at higher levels in the organization. Pointing to inadequacies in leadership research, with regard to a consideration of multiple levels, leadership experts highlight the importance of considering multiple levels of analysis in such research. Thus, performance management models can be enhanced by focusing on the unit or group level of analysis, in addition to the inter-individual or dyadic level of analysis.

The conventional postulation that managers are susceptible to the self-serving attributional bias, if taken to the unit level of analysis, would suggest that they take responsibility for positive behavioral and performance outcomes but deny responsibility for negative behavioral and performance outcomes of their units. As suggested in the earlier section, managers who are not susceptible to biases are more likely to be effective and considered to be more leader-like. Thus managers who actively take responsibility for the unit's performance and thus attribute the causes of poorly performing subordinates to factors that are under their control are more likely to consider actions that they can take to correct performance deficiencies. This reduces uncertainty faced by the subordinates in the unit. Reducing uncertainty for subordinates can be seen as an important distinction between better performance managers and others. Thus, shaping the work environment and the situational factors that are a component of the work environment in a way that does not negatively affect subordinate and unit performance is a key performance management role. Since most subordinates believe that sources of their poor performance exist in the situational factors, performance managers acknowledging this belief are more likely to build positive relationships with their subordinates than others.

Research on attributional biases indicates that the impact of attributional biases is reduced as managers gain knowledge and experience empathy toward subordinates. By actively taking responsibility for poor performing subordinates and planning actions for correcting those performance deficiencies, managers are likely to send positive signals to their subordinates, peers, and their own managers, thus engendering positive perceptions of leadership all around. This is in contrast to assigning blame to subordinates for poor performance by making internal attributions pointed towards subordinates, which is likely to enhance attributional divergence and dissatisfaction.

The underlying argument here is that leaders take responsibility for the performance of their unit and thereby reduce uncertainty and create an environment within which subordinates can achieve high performance. More specifically, effective leaders point fingers at themselves, look within themselves, and find ways to rectify performance deficiencies. Alternatively, they spread the credit for successes to others and obtain appreciation for everyone in the unit. Recently some experts (Repenning and Sterman 2002) have provided evidence that suggests that this reasoning is a serious possibility in organizations experiencing various degrees of success and failure on projects. Analyzing both successful and failed process improvement attempts at one location over a period of time, these experts discovered a pattern of dysfunctional dispositional attributions on the part of managers in the groups belonging to the process improvement project that failed. In the process improvement project that succeeded, on the other hand, they found managers relating their experience of success as a result of switching from these biased attributions to more external attributions (production system problems) for poor performance. Thus, both theoretical and empirical evidence points to the impact of attributions at the unit rather than the interpersonal level of analysis. This discussion leads to the following performance strategy.

Performance Management Strategy 5: Training managers to look within and make self-internal attributions for poor unit performance leads to better development of performance correction strategies.

Corollary: A self-internal attribution for poor unit performance on the part of managers is positively related to leadership perceptions from their unit members.

On the contrary, in situations of success, leaders focus on enhancing the self-efficacy, satisfaction, and motivation of subordinates by spreading the credit for the successes. Comparing realistic versus unrealistic attributions in the context of their integrative attribution model, psychologists (Forsterling and Morgenstern 2002) found that their central theoretical prediction, that is, the relationship between realistic ability assessments and maximizing overall performance was reinforced. While they found support for the argument that it is functional to make more realistic attributions, these psychologists also found that the "classical attributional findings" held true. Specifically, they found that the group with unrealistic positive ability perceptions did not perform worse than the realistically informed groups. The classical attributional findings from achievement attribution research suggests that high-ability self-assessments that lead to switching attributions of failure to external causes from its true causes is associated with persistence and performance. This may result from the prevention of task-irrelevant cognitions and performance debilitating emotions or the occurrence of negative performance-efficacy spirals and thereby exert a facilitative influence on performance. Attributing unit successes to member contributions, although less than completely realistic, can enhance such motivation and efficacy perceptions and thus provide a stronger foundation for more positive future performance, or even positive amplifying loops of efficacy-performance spirals. Such attributions are also likely to enhance attributional convergence, be seen positively by subordinates, who for the most part have "self-esteem enhancing" tendencies, and result in more support and higher perceptions of leadership from them. This leads to the following performance strategy.

> **Performance Management Strategy 6:** When managers attribute unit successes to the unit's members, it leads to higher levels of subordinate satisfaction.

> **Corollary:** When managers attribute unit successes to the unit's members, it leads to higher perceptions of leadership from them.

Manager Behaviors, Subordinate Attitudes, and Leader Effectiveness

Managers' selection of communication behaviors is enhanced as a result of accurate attributions as stated in the previous section. Further, their feedback giving behavior is also likely to be more immediate and short on latency. In addition, attributing poor unit or organizational performance to themselves is also likely to enable leaders to develop integrative strategies for correcting performance deficiencies. All of these behaviors are likely to help the "self-esteem enhancing" tendency of subordinates and thereby contribute positively to the levels of self-efficacy, satisfaction, and motivation of subordinates. Positive levels of these subordinate attitudes are likely to enhance efficacy-performance spirals in the positive direction, thus enhancing subordinate and unit performance, in addition to improving perceptions of leadership, on the basis of uncertainty removal, esteem enhancement, and satisfaction enhancement. This leads us to the next performance strategy.

Performance Management Strategy 7: Training managers to make accurate attributions and engage in positive interactive behaviors results in higher subordinate self-efficacy and satisfaction.

Corollary 1: When managers are low on feedback latency and provide undistorted feedback, it is positively related to subordinate self-efficacy, and satisfaction.

Corollary 2: When managers provide strategies for correcting performance deficiencies, they have more satisfied subordinates with higher self-efficacy.

Corollary 3: Enhanced levels of subordinate self-efficacy and satisfaction as a result lead to higher perceptions of leadership.

The performance management model presented here is based on empirical support for the underlying theoretical model (Lakshman 2007a). Reliable and valid instruments are available for assessment and trainee development, based on this model. This model has implications for performance management, not only at individual and unit levels, but also at higher organizational levels. Attributional complexity training and programmes for improving attributional complexity of managers can be very fruitful and provide tangible benefits in the long run from a wide variety of perspectives, as can be seen from the process model presented.

DISCUSSION

The available knowledge on performance management has focused almost exclusively on either self-serving or other biases of managers and has excluded key variables, such as accuracy of attributions and criteria like leadership effectiveness. Such focus on biases and exclusion of key criteria results in a number of negative consequences, which can lead to an erosion of trust and leadership, as pointed out at the outset. The knowledge-based model of performance management described here has received strong support in empirical tests. Attributional accuracy has emerged as a key variable of this performance management model. All of the strategies outlined here have been found to be backed by strong empirical support. We have found attributionally accurate managers to interact positively in a behavioral sense. These managers were also quicker and less distorting in their feedback giving behaviors. Accurate managers were also better in their development of performance correction strategies. These positive behaviors are strongly related to subordinate satisfaction and through such satisfaction to leadership perceptions.

Managerial knowledge in the form of cause-effect beliefs are strongly related to the development of performance correction strategies and moderately related to positive interactive behaviors and leadership perceptions. In the context of poor performance, accurate attributions are slightly more important for positive interactive behaviors, as is to be expected, because of their increased specificity to the poor performance context. However, the value of managerial knowledge for performance management in general is unquestionable.

The nature of managerial attributions, in terms of taking responsibility for poor performing units and giving credit to team members for unit successes, also relate to satisfaction and leadership perception. Perhaps most important is the strong support for the findings related to non-susceptibility of managers to gender and racial attributional biases. Although such non-susceptibility of the managers to biases were not related to the development of performance correction strategies directly, these were related to subordinate satisfaction and subsequently to leadership perceptions through the path of subordinate satisfaction.

Thus, the knowledge-based model presented here suggests the following performance management strategies. Management of poor performance, according to this model, begins with detailed causal analysis leading to more accurate attributions.

1. Selecting managers high in attributional complexity and training them for in-depth information processing.
2. Training managers to be more accurate in their causal analysis and to engage in higher and more positive levels of interactive behaviors
3. Training managers to verbalize and document their know-ledge in the form of clear cause-effect beliefs.
4. Training managers to be non-susceptible to attribution biases (gender and racial) leads them to develop better performance correction strategies.
5. Training managers to look within and make self-internal attributions for poor unit performance leads to better de-velopment of performance correction strategies.
6. When managers attribute unit successes to the unit's members, it leads to higher levels of subordinate satisfaction.
7. Training managers to make accurate attributions and engage in positive interactive behaviors results in higher subordinate self-efficacy and satisfaction.

This chapter has presented a model that focuses on the process through which managers' attributions lead to their behaviors, which create the positive environment for subordinate performance accomplishment.

12

KNOWLEDGE LEADERSHIP IN THE NOT-FOR-PROFIT WORLD

Community policing is not soft on crime. Community policing is tougher on crime than traditional policing because it's smarter. A good community police officer will make more arrests than the regular beat officer because he or she will get more information.

—**Commissioner Lee Brown**
(In an interview to A. Webber, *HBR*, 1991)

I pledge to you today that we will continue down the path of full inclusion for all our people, and full participation for all our neighborhoods. To me, Neighborhood Oriented Government is more than a phrase. It's the commitment of a lifetime. And we have already made it work, right here in Houston.

—**Mayor Lee Brown**
Inaugural address at Houston, 1998

Another way we help break the gridlock is by using our expertise to help companies with site planning and land management. Information from our species inventory can be invaluable in helping planners site power line, pipelines, construction projects, or roads. A little biological homework beforehand can avert costly delays, lawsuits, and negative public opinion.

—**John Sawhill, CEO of Nature Conservancy**
(In an interview with A. Howard and J. Magretta, *HBR*, 1995)

A s we have seen briefly in an earlier chapter, concepts of Knowledge Management and Knowledge Leadership extend beyond the boundaries of profit making entities. Knowledge leadership is being practiced effectively by Deveshwar at ITC for balancing business needs with those of development and social responsibility. In this chapter, I discuss several cases of knowledge leadership that are clearly in the not-for-profit realm, serving to illustrate that Knowledge Leadership is purely an organizational issue and does not discriminate between profit and non-profit objectives of organizations. The knowledge-based theory of the firm (á la "*The Theory of the Firm*" in neo-classical economics) suggests that organizations can derive a competitive advantage (or alternatively sustained progress and development) if they are effective at creating, sharing, leveraging, and disseminating knowledge. In other words, one of the crucial objectives of organizations is to manage the knowledge that pertains to their core activities and leverage these activities to add value to the multiple stakeholders in society. The cases discussed in this chapter serve to illustrate the use of non-technological knowledge management systems more than the technological knowledge management systems discussed in the case of the e-choupals of ITC. Two of the three cases discussed here focus on urban issues of crime, poverty, and suffering, and the application of knowledge leadership to solving these problems from within a community hospital, and the confines of a police department and city administration. The third case deals with environmental conservation issues handled by the effective knowledge leadership of a non-profit conservancy organization. The case of knowledge leadership provided in two separate instances by Lee Brown, who was first the Commissioner of Police, New York City Police Department (NYPD), and then Mayor of Houston is first described. This is followed by the other instance of urban knowledge leadership, that provided by Tom Chapman at Greater Southeast Community Hospital in Washington D.C. The concluding section of this chapter deals with John Sawhill's knowledge leadership at Nature Conservancy, a not-for-profit organization.

LEE P. BROWN'S KNOWLEDGE LEADERSHIP

As stated earlier, despite decades of research on leadership and the existence of a voluminous literature on the topic, the role of leadership in managing information and knowledge has not been addressed in that literature. More specifically, the role of such leaders in managing information and knowledge in an urban context has received no attention, despite its importance to the vast number of growing cities, burgeoning with unique urban problems, around the world. Mayor Lee Brown of Houston presents an excellent example of an individual who has led his organization by managing knowledge in all his past positions as Mayor of Houston, Commissioner of NYPD, and Chief of Houston Police, among other positions. When he took over as Chief of Police in Houston in 1982, he faced a significant dilemma and an ongoing crisis. Various segments of Houston's population felt alienated and threatened.[1] When he took over as Commissioner of Police in New York City, there was much the same problem of alienation, feelings of being threatened, not to mention the growing crime problem in the city. In 1989, there were 712,419 crimes, including 1,905 murders, 93,777 robberies, and 3,254 rapes in New York City. He perceived the problem to be along the lines of a national health emergency, with the causes deeply rooted in the US social and economic systems.

The Dilemma

He spent a great deal of time drawing on his educational resources, knowledge, and background in searching for solutions to these problems. He was convinced that the traditional policing model of "crime reduction", where cops responded to 911 calls and patrolled the streets in cars could neither respond adequately to the challenge of crime nor could it result in effective management of police resources. However, he still wrestled with the idea of finding a better solution to the problem of crime. He recognized that any solution would result from a true knowledge of the cause of the problem that was so endemic to the urban areas of the country. In this context, again, he was reasonably sure that the "arrest and incarcerate" model of dealing with crime, and the "command and control" model of managing the police force were not the answers to the problem. With a doctorate in criminology from the University of California, Dr Brown had some special insights into the problem of crime and the means to solve those problems. He said:

> Our traditional role is to arrest and incarcerate people, and we are very good at that. We're arresting people in record numbers. In fact, prison overcrowding is the biggest problem in most states. ... The fact is, crime is higher now than ever before and the police know things aren't working. (Webber 1991)

Knowledge: Cause-Effect Beliefs

To Brown, the answer lay in accurately identifying the underlying factors that produce crime and in developing the commitment to deal with them. A fundamental tenet of Knowledge Management is to understand the cause-effect relationships as the means to convert tacit knowledge into explicit knowledge (Saffady 2000). Knowledge Management can result only from such conversion of tacit knowledge to explicit knowledge (Lakshman 2007a). If the true cause of crime was located in social and economic systems, as Brown reasoned it was, then it required a drastically different approach to handling crime, and as a consequence to managing the police department. In managing the crime department, he advocated a new philosophy of community policing, which would target problems in society, by cops walking the beat, building relationships with the community members, getting to know the people, and using the knowledge and information obtained from such sources to solve crime problems and to nab criminals. According to Brown, "Community policing is based on the realization that most crimes are solved with information that comes from people. The better your relationship with the people, the more information you'll get" (Webber 1991).

Brown insisted that community policing should be used as the dominant style of the New York Police Department, in contrast to the traditional policing methods which, he strongly felt, were ineffective at targeting the root cause of crime. Although he also felt that crime and its management was not only a police problem, and that it needed efforts from everyone in society, including government and educators, he did not shy away from the police work of solving crime and nabbing criminals. He wanted police officers in all departments, from detectives to narcotics, not just patrol officers, to operate under the concept of community policing. Under this concept, their work would not be managed by the telephone and responding to 911 calls. A small percentage of people were making these calls that were consuming a vast majority of the resources of the police department. Instead, these officers would actively incorporate the community members in the policing efforts by getting to know them, building relationships with them, getting people to trust and respect them, and, in some cases, organizing the community to ward off crime. Thus, in his mind, community policing would provide the communities with effective means to fight crime, rather than sole reliance on the police and the justice system to do the job.

> Let me give you one example from Houston. We had an officer who tried community policing in a neighborhood where there was a rash of break-ins where the burglars were armed and showed no hesitancy to shoot.... He pulled people together in that community so well that they even gave their neighborhood a name. People handed out flyers describing the pattern of the crimes and what to look for. As a result, one citizen called in because of some suspicious circumstances, and we caught the burglars. Instead of blaming the police, the citizens joined the police. (Webber 1991)

Customer-Focused Knowledge Management

In addition to changing the dominant policing style from "arrest and incarcerate" to community policing, Brown realized that other changes were needed in the organization's culture to implement community policing well enough to be successful. He felt convinced that the "command and control" model of managing the police department was out of touch with reality. By not trusting the officers to be intelligent, creative, and to handle problems with reasonable degrees of the autonomy, the 'command and control' model adopted the paramilitary style of organizational pyramids, rigid lines of reporting, and rules and regulations that cover everything. As an alternative to the traditional "command and control" model of managing the department, he advocated and implemented a model that would be consistent with the concept of community policing, where the cops would be on the beat, the way its used to be when police departments were originally created. These cops would operate under two tenets, namely, problem solving and citizen involvement. With the first tenet of problem solving, the concept of community policing calls for an empowered work force that solves problems without being overly constrained by rules and regulations, and rigid reporting relationships. The other tenet of citizen involvement would expand the resources of the police department, by allowing the customers (citizens) to participate in improvement. Thus, Commissioner Brown was managing knowledge both on the inside and the outside, by engaging in community policing. Recent research suggests that Knowledge Management and customer-focused knowledge management are both required dimensions of the overall concept of managing information and knowledge to solve organizational problems.[2] Brown said, "Just as companies are finding new ways for customers to participate in improvement, we have a virtually untapped resource of community groups, the private sector, and other city agencies, all of which can help us do community problem solving" (Webber 1991).

Knowledge Management and Change

As with any change effort, Brown needed to start from the top of the organization and communicate his vision for change and exchange information and knowledge with people at all levels and all departments in the organization about the new style and the corresponding requirements. "I called them together for weekly meetings of the executive staff. It was the first time they regularly met as a group. As we implement community policing, they will keep their areas of responsibility, but already they're beginning to ask how new initiatives in any area will fit in with the department wide shift" (Webber 1991). Another aspect of Knowledge Management that was used by Commissioner Brown in dealing with the change is by changing the recruitment and hiring process, focusing on bringing in knowledgeable, more educated people, better equipped with problem solving capabilities. He brought in people who understood sociology, the dynamics of people in groups, com-munity problems, and those who could solve problems that defied easy solutions.

In addition to changing the hiring process, Brown also changed the training methods and approaches and used more Knowledge Management approaches such as technology-based knowledge management methods to bring in the changes effectively.

We have to make this part of everyone's training. I am going into every one of our 75 precincts to explain community policing. I'm regularly sending out videotapes that will be played at every roll call, explaining different aspects of community policing. I'm talking to every new class that enters the police academy. When officers are promoted to the Sergeant's class, I talk to the Sergeant's class.... As we implement community policing, we'll use the people who are actually doing it as advocates and experts. They're the ones who know that it works. They're the ones who will improve our current understanding of how to do it. (Webber 1991)

Recent research suggests that such methods are consistent with both the technology and social routes to effective knowledge management. Further, such knowledge management can lead to effective organizational outcomes, such as the reduction of crime, in this case. Brown believed in and implemented the concept of community policing in both positions as Chief of Police in Houston and Commissioner of NYPD, in a way that is consistent with the technology and social routes to knowledge management, and the customer-focused dimension of knowledge management. He has therefore successfully demonstrated knowledge leadership in action at his last position as Mayor of Houston, with the concept of neighborhood-oriented government, as indicated in the opening quote.

Neighborhood-Oriented Government: Knowledge Management as Mayor of Houston

Sixteen years ago, when I took command of the Houston Police Department, we faced a crisis of confidence, in which large sectors of the community felt alienated and even threatened. Mayor Whitmire brought me here as Chief with a clear mandate —a mandate to hold the men and women under my command to the highest standards of conduct, and to build a new foundation of trust between the people of Houston and their police.

We did that, and the tool we used was Neighborhood Oriented Policing. By assigning police to work in the neighborhoods, with community and religious leaders, business owners, educators and private citizens, we built an effective new partnership in the fight against crime. And we broke down the barriers of suspicion and fear that stood in the way of progress.

—Commissioner Lee Brown in his 1998 address to Houstonians

Just as he wanted the community to be involved in policing efforts in his Police Chief and Commissioner roles in two cities, he wanted the people of the city to be involved in the governing of the city, truly adhering to both the concept of democracy and the concept of Knowledge Management. He saw that as the main mechanism to avoid the feelings of alienation on the part of communities in the city and the perceptions of threat they faced. Neighborhood-oriented government is consistent with customer-focused knowledge management just as much as the community policing, with the model involving citizens in communities in both modes of governance.

> I will be holding regular Town Hall meetings throughout the City. They will be in the evening and weekends, when people are free to attend. And I will ask my department heads to join me to hear citizens concerns firsthand. I will make myself available for "Mayors Night In" sessions at City Hall, during which citizens will have the opportunity to meet with me.

Consistent with his cause-effect beliefs associated with the importance of education and knowledge in reducing crime and other problems in cities, he envisioned the possibility of increasing childrens' access to libraries. "My vision is of a Houston in which every child is handed a library card instead of a beer, joint or a pill. Let our kids find their adventures between the covers of a great book, and not the deadly fumes of a crack pipe." In his 1999 state of the city address, he reported that most of the goals he had outlined, organized by five principles into a vision set forth by him the previous year, had been accomplished. He also stated that people were happier, the neighborhoods were safer, and the Houston economy was producing more and more jobs. Areas such as transportation and infrastructure, opportunities for youth and underprivileged, economic development, and productivity improvements in government had all achieved improvements and met goals.[3] He provided an early indication in his new position that his knowledge management methods such as neighborhood-oriented government, and his accurate knowledge of means to improve societies and cities were working.

Pointing to the number of features of neighborhood-oriented government, Mayor Brown said:

Our town hall meetings are resoundingly successful. About 300–400 people attend each meeting, eager to ask questions about city services and facilities and voice their views about how to improve the quality of life in their neighborhoods. Five new satellite courts provide an excellent model of Neighborhood Oriented Government at work by bringing our municipal courts closer to the people, to their communities. Citizens no longer have to come downtown to resolve non-trial matters in municipal court. Contacting the city will be much easier when the new 311 non-emergency phone system becomes effective in about one year. We will be placing kiosks throughout the city, thereby providing a means for conducting some city business in the neighborhoods without going downtown.[4]

All of these methods enriched and strengthened the knowledge-based strategies for governance that were part of his policing approaches as commissioner.

He continued to think about challenges in the future, such as demands on transportation with future population growth in the city, clean air requirements, water supply requirements, and business growth. He continued to address these challenges with solutions that targeted the roots of the problems in his inimitable style of identifying cause-effect relations and developing consistent solutions. To further enhance the involvement of citizens in the city's government, he initiated the concept of super neighborhood councils.

Our Super Neighborhood councils have brought together neighborhoods to speak with one voice, sometimes a very loud voice. The department heads have joined me many times in meeting with the Councils as they work on their Super Neighborhood Action Plans. This hasn't just been a public relations effort. The Councils have been a valuable part of the Capital Improvement Planning process. They know what they need and it is our job to deliver.[5]

Through all of the additional responsibilities brought on by the position of Mayor, Brown realized the importance of and delivered on the safety of the citizens through the police department that was and is so dear to his heart.

Protecting our citizens is the foremost responsibility of municipal government. That has been and will continue to be the top priority of my administration. Having devoted my career to law enforcement, I know a good police department when I see one. The men and women of the Houston Police Department are the most professional and dedicated I have had the pleasure to work with. In 2001, we opened two new police storefront stations and broke ground for another—bringing our total to 31. We added two helicopters to our fleet, as well as a Cessna airplane....[6]

Mayor Brown continued to use his concepts of neighborhood-oriented policing and government and use both people and technology in implementing his actions, consistent with both knowledge management and customer-focused knowledge management dimensions. These Knowledge Management concepts and their governance applications are popular with the people as evidenced by their effectiveness and their re-election of Mayor Brown to three successive terms in office. Mayor Brown exemplifies leadership of a nature that is on the cutting edge.

TOM CHAPMAN'S KNOWLEDGE LEADERSHIP

In 1991 Tom Chapman became CEO of Greater Southeast Community Hospital, a 494-bed acute care facility located in Washington D.C. It had an employee strength of 2,650 employees and revenues of US$145 million, by virtue of which it was the largest private employer in the troubled and isolated community of Anacostia. Low levels of education, unrelenting poverty, and unique inner-city problems gave Anacostia the highest rates of infant mortality, cancer, and coronary disease in the Washington D.C. area. Tom Chapman's effective leadership shows in the continued success and prosperity of the hospital in the face of other inner-city hospitals facing severe operating losses and closure. His approach to the leadership of the community hospital, driven by an innate understanding of inner-city needs (he grew up in such an environment), is fairly unique and demonstrates the successful use of Knowledge Leadership concepts. His cause-effect beliefs for solving huge inner-city problems and the subsequent reshaping of the hospital's mission, and utilization of various teams within the organization are all critical elements of his knowledge leadership.

Knowledge: Cause-Effect Beliefs

Under Chapman's leadership, the hospital has renovated housing, started day care programs for children and the elderly, developed stay-in-school programs, and created adult literacy programs. Many people looking at this list of programs would wonder what a hospital is doing establishing and running these programs. This is where Chapman's (cause-effect) beliefs about what is truly required to keep the hospital sustainable and provide tangible benefits to the community in which it operates were critical and instrumental in leading to the success of this hospital in the face of failure of many other similar hospitals. He believed, for one, that the hospital should be self-sustaining and not give away too much of its services to people that were uninsured. This would ensure that the hospital could sustain itself, unlike the many others that had failed to survive to provide services to the community. He also believed that there was no use in treating symptoms of larger social problems manifesting themselves as pneumonia or gunshot wounds, and so on. He believed that the fundamental answer to these problems lay in diagnosing and treating the real diseases that were racking the community. In his words:

> We can take care of the symptoms surprisingly well. We sew up gunshot wounds and administer antibiotics, but we aren't dealing with the violence on the streets or the fact that we have to discharge a child to a cold apartment (which may lead to recurrence of pneumonia). Those are the real diseases that are racking our community. Our Health care costs will continue to skyrocket until we start to deal with these problems. Our hospital does a miraculous job of keeping very sick fragile infants alive. Yet most of that incredibly expensive care should be unnecessary. With good nutrition, proper prenatal care, decent housing, and a little bit of education, most deliveries can be low-cost, joyous events. (Nichols 1992)

Other hospitals were probably aware of these factors but quite possibly were not sure how to respond to the challenges posed by the community problems.

Chapman challenges conventional knowledge and wisdom by suggesting that the hospital's margins were inextricably linked to its mission. More importantly, it was important to reshape that mission to make the hospital viable and continue on its path of providing valuable services to meet the real needs of community members. He believed in what he said:

> You have to think beyond the walls of the hospital and get beyond technology and what it can do. Simply staying in the shop and providing good emergency care without thinking about what happens before our patients arrive and after they leave is a tremendous waste of resources. For instance, by saving low-weight and drug-addicted babies, we may actually be adding to society's problems. (Nichols 1992)

In addition to preventive care to treat many physical ills, he also believed that it was essential to treat the social ills with appropriate solutions, in the absence of any such mechanisms in society to deal with them. In the absence of such effort, he foresaw the skyrocketing of costs for the hospital, eventually running it down, as evidenced in the case of many other hospitals in the area.

He believed, argued for, and put in an action plan to bring about true focus on the needs of community members (customers), as opposed to the conventional way of focusing on provider needs. Instead of running a health clinic that is closed after 5 p.m. and on weekends, Greater Southeast opened clinics in high schools and in middle schools, where the children can be monitored for major problems and treated for minor problems, which would otherwise end up in the high-cost emergency room. In addition to such clinics, Greater Southeast helped renovate housing, provided elderly day care out of the basement of their hospital, and established stay-in-school and adult literacy programs, which are typically not within the mission of most hospitals. Having reshaped the mission of the hospital, and having put in a number of preventive measures at schools and volunteer groups at churches and other community locations for screening purposes, Chapman turned his attention to within the organization.

Chapman's knowledge leadership on the inside came through the creation of employee volunteering programs where they would feed recovering patients during their lunch hour (saving costs and building motivation), building learning communities among nurses and other employees to solve organizational problems, and by organizing patient-focused team of cross-functional employees. Speaking on the volunteer programs, Chapman says:

> We've found that the clerical employees who are detached from the caring mission of the hospital like being involved in this nursing activity. They find it fulfilling. From the hospital's perspective, the program saves both time and money. We don't have to pay a highly trained nurse to perform a routine feeding, and we don't have lengthened stays brought on by infections resulting from the feeding tubes. The patients also benefit physically and mentally from the added nutrition and from the extra social contact. (Nichols 1992)

Chapman built learning communities by organizing weekly meetings with nurses and other employees, encouraging them to submit problems along with their solutions, rather than simply reporting the complaints. The requirement of solutions turned these meetings into vibrant learning communities (á la quality circles) and the nurses showed improvement over a period of time.

> One of the first things I did when I got here was oversee the renovation of each of eight nursing stations, one on each floor of the hospital. I gave each nursing team the responsibility of designing its area. The nurses loved it, and as we went up floor by floor, each renovation became more cost-effective—because they were learning from each other as the process went on. (Nichols 1992)

Moving the concept of customer-focused knowledge management forward, Chapman instituted cross-functional teams of employees focused on the patient. These teams help serve the most crucial and salient needs of the patient, which may vary from time to time.

Each elderly patient is treated by a geriatric team that includes a doctor, a nurse, a social worker, a dietician, and a physical therapist. In effect the patient picks the team leader. If the patient's most critical needs are emotional, then the social worker leads the team—not the doctor. (Nichols 1992)

Thus, such teams could gather real-time information from the patients and provide for those needs accordingly, which facilitates the providing of an integrated healthcare system. The combined impact of all of the aforementioned knowledge leadership efforts resulted in net 'profits' for the organization, which were turned around and invested in the community. This investment has come in the form of expansion from a single acute care hospital into a network of community-based entities: two hospitals, three nursing homes, and a multitude of ambulatory programs for elderly people, children, and their families. Such communities are more than lucky to have such knowledge leaders running critical organizations.

JOHN SAWHILL AT NATURE CONSERVANCY

Having dealt with two cases of urban knowledge leadership, I now turn my attention to a different kind of social responsibility, namely, environmental conservation. John Sawhill became the CEO of Nature Conservancy, the largest conservation organization in the world, in 1990. The Nature Conservancy manages 1,600 separate preserves from more than 200 offices spread from Maine to Micronesia, with about US$1 billion in assets. John Sawhill's leadership has been very instrumental in bringing about rapid growth to the conservancy. John Sawhill has utilized knowledge leadership to bring about change in the organization, which according to him was very instrumental to accomplish the mission. More importantly, he felt that the organization's mission was critical in guiding change in the organization. The conservancy's mission has always been to preserve plants and animals and special habitats that represent the diversity of life. One of the first things that Sawhill sensed was going wrong was the fact that although the number of acres under protection was increasing, actual preservation was not being accomplished.

> In the past, whenever we wanted to know how we were doing, we could simply count the acres we'd protected and check our membership figures. Those measures weren't giving us the right information. We had a terrific collection of preserves, but there was growing concern about the lasting effectiveness of our conservation strategy. Places we thought were protected really weren't. (Howard and Magretta 1995)

The total acres under protection had increased from 2.3 million in 1985 to 8.14 million in 1995. Total membership in Nature Conservancy had also increased from 533,113 in 1989 to 818,000 in 1995. By these traditional measures, the conservancy was accomplishing its objectives. However, something was missing. The mission of preserving plants, animals, and threatened habitats was not being accomplished, evidenced by the decline in the population of endangered species in the protected lands.

Cause-Effect Beliefs as Knowledge

Sawhill noticed that the numbers of the endangered species in the lands that were purchased and set aside for preservation purposes were actually going down. He brought his special knowledge and understanding of the situation to bear on this problem. He identified that activities that were taking place outside of the protected lands owned by the conservancy, but in the vicinity of those lands, were affecting the preservation mission. In Sawhill's words:

> Our experience with Schenob Brook in Massachusetts, for example, helped to alert us. A number of years after we had acquired that property, we were alarmed to find that the bog turtle population was declining. It turned out that activities outside our preserve were affecting the water that the turtles ultimately depended on. (Howard and Magretta 1995)

Thus, simply buying parcels of land and fencing it off was no longer sufficient. Based on such analysis, Sawhill was able to provide the solution of buying larger pieces of land in each location to minimize the impact of external activities on life inside the preserve. Additionally, he also started undertaking an initiative of managing the process of educating people in the immediate vicinity of the preserve, where further land acquisition was not possible, in the potential damage their activities could cause to life inside the preserve. Thus, the broader management of the stakeholders, including education and training of those in the vicinity, were becoming increasingly important. The fundamental realization however, is that the traditional measure of adding up acres of land under protection was too simplistic and not helping in achievement of the mission.

Sawhill also had clear and firm beliefs on problems within the organization that were contributing to non-achievement of the mission. Sawhill's explicit knowledge of the fact that he was heading a knowledge organization populated by knowledge workers was the key to the recognition that such knowledge needed to be shared, leveraged, and disseminated. He noticed many problems in this regard.

> Some of the basic systems we were using to run the enterprise hadn't kept up with the rapid growth. Our financial system was not producing reports on time, our marketing system was not giving us accurate, up-to-date information on our members, and our personnel systems were antiquated. In addition, the board of governors was concerned that the organization was becoming fragmented. It needed leadership, it needed to be pulled together, it needed to have a clear vision of where it was going. (Howard and Magretta 1995)

He was very concerned about the fact that successful integration of the scientific information with the conservation planning and executing work was not adequate. He conceived of two businesses that the conservancy was basically involved in. One was the science driven organization that depended on maintaining the world's

best databases on species and their habitats and provided information on threatened areas to insiders and outsiders such as
government agencies and corporations. This business was to be
integrated with the business of buying land and protecting it. He
realized that the successful integration of these two businesses would
entail stewardship capabilities and a non-confrontational approach
to all the key stakeholders involved in the process. For instance:

> If an oil company wants to drill in an environmentally sensitive area, we
> won't say: Don't drill. Instead we ask, Is there any way you can drill and
> not harm the area's ecological integrity? Let's try to develop a drilling plan
> that won't disturb the wildlife habitat. We believe in partnerships. (Howard
> and Magretta 1995)

Thus, he was able to provide the knowledge required to various
organizations involved and bring about mitigation solutions that
would satisfy multiple needs. He envisioned and brought about
a change whereby the Nature Conservancy became a knowledge
storehouse and provided assistance to corporations that were
interested in achieving economic objectives without harming
ecological objectives.

Organizational Solutions

For this, he first had to provide an organizational solution for lack
of integration of financial, marketing, and personnel information.
He created learning communities within the organization that
would work on their core competence, that is, knowledge. He constituted a strategy task force comprising four of the most capable
up-and-coming managers of the organization. "Those four are still
with the organization and they're all in key leadership roles today. I
tried to have some balance in expertise and in geography: We had
two scientists, one fund-raiser, and one person who was involved
in land acquisition" (Howard and Magretta 1995). Fund raising
to purchase land that could then be protected was a key ingredient
of the operations of this non-profit organization. This task

force, with Sawhill, worked on strategic planning for about four months, meeting with different groups that were part of the conservancy: state directors, chapter trustees, and the board. They conducted a series of informational meetings around the country for volunteers and staff, apprising them of the organization's mission and strategy and leveraging knowledge in the process. He also constituted a conservation committee and an operations committee and formulated them as part of the larger learning communities within the organization. Thus was formed the broad socio-cognitive network of knowledge that supplemented the technological network, that is, the databases and knowledge bases on species, habitats, wetlands, and so on.

> Our task force conducted about 75 interviews all over the organization, which helped bring to the surface many of the ideas and concerns that had been floating around. It also interviewed outsiders, including scientists and people in other conservation organizations. After five months of discussions, the organization coalesced around the new strategy of larger landscapes as well as a variety of new challenges, including riskier conservation strategies. (Howard and Magretta 1995)

Thus, the socio-cognitive network helped bring to the surface the tacit knowledge that was available with multiple sources inside and outside and in its eventual conversion into actionable explicit knowledge.

The conservation committee, part of the broader effort in establishing learning communities within the organization, was established to discuss and debate issues affecting our mission. The operations committee was established to handle administration issues. Both of these committees were formed by taking a vertical slice of the organization and bringing in people from various organizational levels together. A third entity, in the form of a management council, comprising roughly 150 managers from all parts of the organization, was also established as part of the larger initiative. Unlike the other two committees, the management council was designed to meet once a year to review the work done by those two committees. Thus, significant changes were made to the organizational structure to enable smooth flow of information and knowledge and thereby integrate the organization and make it ready to meet challenges from the outside. In Sawhill's words, "The new structure replaces a tighter management team that had consisted only of senior staff, and it represents a real shift in management philosophy. The early returns are positive" (Howard and Magretta 1995). The overall objective was to increase creativity, provide non-regulatory solutions to environmental issues, reduce bureaucracy, and increase the knowledge-orientation within the organization. These efforts were crucial in terms of their capabilities to provide assistance to organizations, such as Walt Disney Corporation and the Georgia Pacific Company by providing knowledge solutions to their environmental problems.

> In 1992, the Walt Disney Company wanted to expand its operations in Orlando, Florida, to build its wild animal theme park. The State, however, was concerned about damage to wetlands. A solution was jointly engineered by Disney, the Nature Conservancy, and local, state, and federal agencies: In exchange for permission to develop the Orlando site, which will affect about 340 acres of wetlands over a 20-year period, Disney agreed to purchase, protect, and restore 8,500 acres of wetlands and wilderness in central Florida. Disney will donate this land in phases to the Conservancy and provide an endowment to make sure that we can continue to operate it. (Howard and Magretta 1995)

An example where the conservancy used its expertise to help companies in site planning and land management is their work with the Georgia-Pacific Corporation, which wanted to consider how it might contribute to conservation but not give up all its rights to harvest timber in perpetuity on a particular piece of property. Using its knowledge the Conservancy suggested which areas can be logged, which need to be set aside on a permanent basis, and entered into an agreement with the Conservancy that gives equal rights to both organizations in determining future timber harvests. Thus Georgia-Pacific was able to attain its economic objective without losing public reputation on the environmental count.

Thus Sawhill's knowledge leadership in integrating the information and knowledge within the organization using both the technological and social routes has immensely helped the organization in achieving its basic mission of protecting plants, animals, and threatened habitats. Peter Drucker had once referred to the Nature Conservancy as the best example of a winning strategy in a non-profit institution. John Sawhill, through his knowledge leadership and by changing the organization significantly during his tenure ensured that what Drucker had once said remained true for years to come. He noticed the problems, reshaped the mission and the organization, keeping the mission firmly in mind, and converted the conservancy into an organization that created, leveraged, and harvested knowledge that was so critical to its success.

NOTES

1. L. Brown (1998). Inaugural address to the City of Houston.
2. C. Lakshman (2007a). See also Alavi and Leidner (2001) for the foundation of these concepts.
3. L. Brown (1999). State of the City address to Houstonians.
4. L. Brown (2000). State of the City address.
5. L. Brown (2002). Inaugural address to Houston.
6. L. Brown (2002). State of the City address.

BIBLIOGRAPHY

Agres, Ted. 1991. "Asea Brown Boveri—A Model for Global Management", *Research & Development*. Available online at http://findarticles.com/p/articles/mi_hb3386/is_199112/ai_n8134524?tag=artBody;col1 (downloaded June 2008).

Alavi, M. and D.E. Leidner. 2001. "Knowledge Management and Knowledge Management Systems: Conceptual foundations and research issues", *MIS Quarterly*, 25(1): 107–36.

Appropriate Technology. 2005. "Indian Farmers Gain from Internet Access", *Appropriate Technology*, 32(4): 24–31.

Armstrong, C.P. and V. Sambamurthy. 1999. "Information Technology Assimilation in Firms: The Influence of Senior Leadership and IT Structures", *Information Systems Research*, 10(4): 304–27.

Arndt, Michael. 2002. "Quality Isn't Just for Widgets", *Business Week*, July 22. Available online at http://www.businessweek.com/magazine/content/02_29/b3792097.htm (downloaded June 2008).

Asiamoney. 2003/04. www.asiamoney.com, December 2003/January 2004 (downloaded on September 30, 2007).

Asiaweek. 2000. "The Asiaweek 1000: The Old and the New: Li & Fung Looks like an E-commerce Winner", *Asiaweek*, Hong Kong, November 10.

Bilefsky, Dan and Anita Raghavan. 2003. "Blown Fuse: How 'Europe's GE' And Its Star CEO Tumbled to Earth—Percy Barnevik's Leadership Made ABB a Global Name, But Also May Have Hurt It—Lingering Asbestos Woes", *Wall Street Journal* (Eastern edition). New York, January 23.

Booth, Jason. 2001. "Li & Fung Takes Middleman Role to Extremes", *Asian Wall Street Journal*, Hong Kong, December 14.

Burns, J.M. 1978. *Leadership*. New York: Harper & Row.

Business Line. 2002. "ITC E-choupals to Cover 1 Lakh Villages within a Decade", *Business Line*, Chennai, December 4.

———. 2004a. "Give Them Empowerment First", Chennai, November 19.

———. 2004b. "Ryot Choice", *Business Line*, Chennai, November 26.

———. 2004c. "Soya Trading Grinds to Halt on Mandi Stir: Traders Protest Against E-Choupal", *Business Line*, Chennai, December 17.

———. 2005a. "ITC Wins 'Golden Peacock' Award", *Business Line*, Chennai, May 17.

———. 2005b. "ITC's E-choupal Bags TERI Award", *Business Line*, Chennai, June 3.

———. 2005c. "Rewarding Resourcefulness, Lifting Lives", *Business Line*, Chennai, July 2.

———. 2005d. "Village Knowledge Centres Vital for Rural Development", *Business Line*, Chennai, July 12.

Business Line. 2006a. "ITC to Invest $1 Billion in E-choupal Infrastructure", *Business Line*, Chennai, January 4.

———. 2006b. "Lintas Media Arm, E-choupal Join to Launch Bharat Barometer", *Business Line*, Chennai, August 9.

———. 2006c. "ITC Aims to Cover 1 lakh Villages thru e-choupal: Helps Farmers to Access Crop Specific Real-time Information", *Business Line*, Chennai, August 26.

———. 2006d. "Full of Plans", *Business Line*, Chennai, October 12.

———. 2007a. "E-choupal, a Novel Private Sector Initiative: Survey", *Business Line*, Chennai, February 26.

———. 2007b. "E-choupal, A Novel Private Sector Initiative: Survey", *Business Line*, Chennai, February 28.

———. 2007c. "Marketing: Dukes expanding in Northern, Eastern Regions", *Business Line*, Chennai, May 2.

———. 2007d. "ITC E-choupals to Focus on Product Traceability", *Business Line*, Chennai, August 26.

Business Times Singapore. 2005. "A Business Family", *Business Times Singapore*, Singapore, July 23.

Business Wire. 2000. "Dell Extends Lead in Corporate Customer Satisfaction as Competitors Fall Back", *Business Wire*, New York, September 7.

———. 2004. "Gilat Satellite Networks Announces Milestone in ITC-IBD 'E-choupal' Project in India", *Business Wire*, New York, May 3.

Byrne, J.A. 1998. "How Jack Welch Runs GE: A Close-up Look at How America's #1 Manager Runs GE", *Businessweek*, June 8. Available online at http://www.businessweek.com/1998/23/b3581001.htm (downloaded June 2008).

Cleveland, H. 1985. *The Knowledge Executive.* New York: E.P. Dutton.

Collingwood, H. and D.L. Coutu. 2002. "Jack on Jack", *Harvard Business Review*, 80(February, 2): 88–94.

Colvin, Geoffrey. 1999. "The Ultimate Manager", *Fortune*, 140(10): 185–87.

Dammerman, Dennis. 1998. Durland Memorial Lecture, Cornell University, New York, April 1.

Davenport, T.H., D.W. De Long, and M.C. Beers. 1998. "Successful Knowledge Management Projects", *Sloan Management Review*, 39 (Winter, 2): 43–57.

Day, D.V. and R.G. Lord. 1988. "Executive Leadership and Organizational Performance: Suggestions for a New Theory and Methodology," *Journal of Management*, 14(3): 453–64.

Dobbins, G.H. and J.M. Russell. 1986. "Self-Serving Biases in Leadership: A Laboratory Experiment", *Journal of Management*, 12(4): 475–83.

Dobbins, G.H., E.C. Pence, J.A. Orban, and J.A. Sgro. 1983. "The Effects of Sex of the Leader and Sex of the Subordinate on the Use of Organizational Control Policy", *Organizational Behavior and Human Performance*, 32: 325–43.

Dyer, J.H. and K. Nobeoka. 2000. "Creating and Managing a High-performance Knowledge-sharing Network: The Toyota Case", *Strategic Management Journal*, 21(3): 345–67.

Finance Asia. 2004. "Asia's Best Companies", *Finance Asia*, Hong Kong, March 4.

Financial Times. 2003. "HK John Waynes on New Battlefield", *Financial Times*, London, August 30.

Financial World. 1993. "Customer Service: General Electric", *Financial World*, London, September 28.

Fleishman, E.A., M.D. Mumford, S.J. Zaccaro, K.Y. Levin, A.L. Korotkin, and M.B. Hein. 1991. "Taxonomic Efforts in the Description of Leader Behavior: A Synthesis and Functional Interpretation", *Leadership Quarterly*, 2(4): 245–87.

Fletcher, G.J., P. Danilovics, D.P. Fernandez, and G.D. Reeder. 1986. "Attributional Complexity: An Individual Differences Measure", *Journal of Personality and Social Psychology*, 51(4): 875–84.

Fletcher, G.J., G.D. Reeder, and V. Bull. 1990. "Bias and Accuracy in Attitude Attribution: The Role of Attributional Complexity", *Journal of Experimental Social Psychology*, 26(4): 275–88.

Fletcher, G.J., J. Rosanowski, G. Rhodes, and C. Lange. 1993. "Accuracy and Speed of Causal Processing: Experts versus Novices in Social Judgment", *Journal of Experimental Social Psychology*, 28(4): 320–38.

Fokstuen, Anne. 1998. "Tough Times Highlight Li & Fung Model—Trading Company's Success is a Beacon for Family Business in Asia", *Asian Wall Street Journal*, Hong Kong, July 21.

Forsterling, F. and M. Morgenstern. 2002. "Accuracy of Self-Assessment and Task Performance: Does It Pay to Know the Truth?", *Journal of Educational Psychology*, 94(3): 576–85.

Gavin, M.B., S.G. Green, and G.T. Fairhurst. 1995. "Managerial Control Strategies for Poor Performance Over Time and the Impact on Subordinate Reactions", *Organizational Behavior & Human Decision Processes*, 63(2): 207–21.

GE. 1981. *GE Annual Report 1981*, Connecticut.

———. 1989. *GE Annual Report 1989*, Connecticut.

———. 1998. *GE Annual Report 1998*, Connecticut.

———. 1999. *GE Annual Report 1999*, Connecticut.

———. 2000. *GE Annual Report 2000*, Connecticut.

———. 2001. *GE Annual Report 2001*, Connecticut.

Gist, M.E. and T.R. Mitchell. 1992. "Self-Efficacy: A Theoretical Analysis of its Determinants and Malleability", *Academy of Management Review*, 17(2): 183–211.

Green, S.G. and T.R. Mitchell. 1979. "Attributional Processes of Leaders in Leader-Member Interactions", *Organizational Behavior and Human Performance*, 23: 429–58.

Gross, Daniel. 2003. "Do They Know Jack?: Jack Welch's Disciples Have Gone Forth to Preach His Gospel. So Far, Most of Them are Failing", *Slate*, March 4. Available online at http://slate.msn.com/id/2079650/ (downloaded 14 May 2003).

Hansen, M.T., N. Nohria, and T. Tierney. 1999. "What's Your Strategy for Managing Knowledge?", *Harvard Business Review*, 77 (March–April, 2): 106–16.

Herald Tribune. 2007. "Li & Fung Gains Rise with Acquisitions", *Herald Tribune*, New York, August 15.

Hofheinz, Paul. 1993. "Europe's Tough New Managers", *Fortune*, 128(5): 111–14.

Holstein, W.J. 2002. "Middleman Becomes Master: Wal-Mart Watch Out—Giant Hong Kong Trader Li & Fung Boasts an Information System to Beat", *Chief Executive*, October. Available online at http://findarticles.com/p/articles/mi_m4070/is_2002_Oct/ai_93207319 (downloaded June 2008).

Holstein, W.J. 2003. "Dell: One Company, Two CEO's: Michael Dell Knew He Couldn't Manage Alone. So He's Struck a Partnership with Kevin Rollins—Related Article: Dell on Dell's Future—Interview—Company Profile—Cover Story", *The Chief Executive*, November. Available online at http://findarticles.com/p/articles/mi_m4070/is_193/ai_110811913 (downloaded June 2008).

Hong, Y., C. Chiu, C.S. Dweck, D. M.-S. Lin and W. Wan. 1999. "Implicit Theories, Attributions, and Coping: A Meaning System Approach", *Journal of Personality and Social Psychology*, 77(3): 588–99.

House, R.J. and R.N. Aditya. 1997. "The Social Scientific Study of Leadership: Quo Vadis?", *Journal of Management*, 23(3): 409–73.

Howard, A. and J. Magretta, 1995. "Surviving Success: An Interview with the Nature Conservancy's John Sawhill", *Harvard Business Review (HBR)*, 73 (September–October, 5): 109–18.

Kalam, A.P.J. 2007. "Agriculture Cannot Wait: New Horizons", Special address during the National Symposium of commemorate 60 years of Independence, New Delhi, June 5, 2007. Available online at http://www.itcportal.com/news room/press 06 june 07-a.htm.

Kelley, H.H. 1972. "Attribution in Social Interactions", in E.E. Jones, D.E. Kanouse, H.H. Kelley, R.E. Nisbett, S. Valins and B. Weiner (eds), *Attributions: Perceiving the Causes of Behavior*, pp. 1–26. Morristown, New Jersey: General Learning Press.

Kleinman, Mark. 2007. "Marks and Spencer's British Shoe Supplier Sold to Li & Fung of Hong Kong". Available online at http://www.telegraph.co.uk/money/main.jhtml?xml=/money/2007/08/16/cnmarks116.xml (downloaded on September 30, 2007).

Knight Ridder/Tribune News. 2007. "Firdose Vandrevala Quits Motorola", *Knight Ridder/Tribune News*, Chennai, June 12.

Knowlton, W.A. and T.R. Mitchell. 1980. "Effects of Causal Attributions on a Supervisor's Evaluation of Subordinate Performance", *Journal of Applied Psychology*, 65(4): 459–66.

Kuttayan Annamalai and Sachin Rao. 2003. "What Works: ITC's E-choupal and Profitable Rural Transformation," Case Study Series, University of Michigan. Available online at http://www.nextbillion.net/files/eChoupal.pdf (downloaded June 2008).

Lakshman, C. 2005. "Top Executive Knowledge Leadership: Managing Knowledge to Lead Change at General Electric", *Journal of Change Management*, 5(4): 429–46.

———. 2007a. "Organizational Knowledge Leadership: A Grounded Theory Approach", *Leadership and Organization Development Journal*, 28(1): 51–75.

———. 2007b. "The Role of Attributions and Attributional Accuracy in Managing Subordinate Performance: The Indian Context", *International Journal of Indian Culture and Business Management*, 1(1/2): 83–103.

Larson, J.R. 1989. "The Dynamic Interplay Between Employees' Feedback-Seeking Strategies and Supervisors' Delivery of Performance Feedback", *Academy of Management Review*, 14(3): 408–22.

Lee-Young, J. and M. Barnett. 2001. "Furiously Fast Fashions", *Industry Standard Magazine*, San Francisco, June 11: 72–79.

Levinson, M. 2000. "Destructive Behavior", *CIO Magazine*, July 15. Available online at http://www.cio.com/archive/071500_destructive.html (downloaded May 12, 2003).

Li & Fung. 2007. www.lifunggroup.com (downloaded on September 30, 2007).

Liden, R.C. and T.R. Mitchell. 1985. "Reactions to Feedback: The Role of Attributions", *Academy of Management Journal*, 28(2): 291–308.

Liden, R.C., G.R. Ferris and R.M. Dienesch. 1988. "The Influence of Causal Feedback on Subordinate Reactions and Behavior", *Group & Organization Studies*, 13(3): 348–73.

Lindsley, D.H., D.J. Brass and J.B. Thomas. 1995. Efficacy-Performance Spirals: A Multilevel Perspective", *Academy of Management Review*, 20(3): 645–78.

Lord, R.G. and J.E. Smith. 1983. "Theoretical, Information Processing, and Situational Factors Affecting Attribution Theory Models of Organizational Behavior", *Academy of Management Review*, 8(3): 50–60.

Lord, R.G. and K.J. Maher. 1991. *Leadership and Information Processing: Linking Perceptions and Performance*. Boston: HarperCollins.

Luthans, F., K.W. Luthans, R.M. Hodgetts, and B.C. Luthans. 2002. "Positive Approach to Leadership (PAL): Implications for Today's Organizations", *The Journal of Leadership Studies*, 8(2): 3–20.

Magretta, J. 1998. "The Power of Virtual Integration: An Interview with Dell Computer's Michael Dell", *Harvard Business Review (HBR)*, 76(March–April, 2): 73–84.

———. 1998. "Fast, Global, and Entrepreneurial: Supply Chain Management, Hong Kong Style: An Interview with Victor Fung", *Harvard Business Review (HBR)*, 76(September–October, 5): 103–14.

Martinko, M.J. and W.L. Gardner. 1982. "Learned Helplessness: An Alternative Explanation for Performance Deficits", *Academy of Management Review*, 7(2): 195–204.

———. 1987. "The Leader/Member Attribution Process", *Academy of Management Review*, 12(2): 235–49.

McClenahen, John S. 1994. "Percy Barnevik and the ABBs of Competition", *Industry Week*, Cleveland, June 6.

McGinn, Daniel. 2000. "Jack Welch Goes Surfing: Nearing Retirement GE's Chief Has Become a Net Evangelist, His Homily: The Web is Best Used to Rewire Old Companies, not Start New Ones", *Newsweek*, December 25. Available online at http://www.newsweek.com/id/104973/page/1 (downloaded June 2008).

Miller, D., M.F.R. Kets de Vries and J. Toulouse. 1982. "Locus of Control and Its Relationship to Strategy, Environment, and Structure", *Academy of Management Journal*, 25: 237–53.

Mintzberg, H. 1973. *The Nature of Managerial Work*. New York: Harper and Row.

Mitchell, T.R. and L.S. Kalb. 1982. "Effects of Job Experience on Supervisor Attributions for a Subordinate's Poor Performance", *Journal of Applied Psychology*, 67(April): 181–88.

Mitchell, T.R. and R.E. Wood. 1980. "Supervisor's Responses to Subordinate Poor Performance: A Test of an Attributional Model", *Organizational Behavior and Human Performance*, 25: 123–38.

Mitchell, T.R., S.G. Green, and R.E. Wood. 1981. "An Attributional Model of Leadership and the Poor Performing Subordinate: Development and Validation", in

L.L. Cummings and B.M. Staw (eds), *Research in Organizational Behavior*, Volume 3, pp. 197–234. Greenwich, Connecticut: JAI Press.

Moss, S.E. and M.J. Martinko. 1998. "The Effects of Performance Attributions and Outcome Dependence on Leader Feedback Behavior following Poor Subordinate Performance", *Journal of Organizational Behavior*, 19: 259–74.

Murphy, R. 1999. "Michael Dell", *Success*, January.

Nichols, N.A. 1992. "Profits with a Purpose: An Interview with Tom Chapman", *Harvard Business Review (HBR)*, 70 (November–December, 6): 86–95.

Nichols, Nancy 1994. "Medicine, Management, and Mergers: An Interview with Merck's P. Roy Vagelos," *Harvard Business Review (HBR)*, 72(November–December, 6): 105–14.

Nonaka, I. and H. Takeuchi. 1995. *The Knowledge Creating Company*. New York: Oxford University Press.

Offermann, L.R., C.J. Schroyer, and S.K. Green. 1998. "Leader Attributions For Subordinate Performance: Consequences for Subsequent Leader Interactive Behaviors and Ratings", *Journal of Applied Social Psychology*, 28(13): 1125–39.

PC World Online. 1999. "Dell Tops Customer Satisfaction Survey". Available online at http://www.pcworld.com/article/9520/dell_tops_customer_satisfaction_survey. html (downloaded on October 1, 2007).

Phillips, J.S. and R.G. Lord. 1981. "Causal Attributions and Perceptions of Leadership", *Organizational Behavior and Human Performance*, 28: 143–63.

Podsakoff, P.M. and D.W. Organ. 1986. "Self-Reports in Organizational Research: Problems and Prospects", *Journal of Management*, 12(4): 531–44.

Prokesch, S.E. 1993. "Mastering Chaos at the High-Tech Frontier: An Interview with Silicon Graphics Edward McCracken", *Harvard Business Review (HBR)*, 71(November–December, 6): 135–144.

———. 1995. "Competing on Customer Service: An Interview with British Airways' Sir Colin Marshall", *Harvard Business Review (HBR)*, 73(November–December, 6): 101–12.

———. 1997. "Unleashing the Power of Learning: An Interview with British Petroleum's John Browne", *Harvard Business Review (HBR)*, 75(September–October, 5): 147–68.

Ramachandran. G. 2004. "Broadband Versus Narrow Elitism", *Business Line*, Chennai, December 28.

Repenning, N.P. and J.D. Sterman. 2002. "Capability Traps and Self-Confirming Attribution Errors in the Dynamics of Process Improvement", *Administrative Science Quarterly*, 47: 265–95.

Rudnitsky, Howard. 2000. "Changing the Corporate DNA", *Forbes*, 166(2): 38–40.

Saffady, W. 2000. "Knowledge Management: An Overview", *The Information Management Journal*, 34(3): 4–8.

Serwer, Andy. 2001. "A Rare Skeptic takes on the Cult of GE", *Fortune*, 143(4): 237–38.

Sillars, A.L. 1981. "Attributions and Interpersonal Conflict-Resolution", in J.H. Harvey, W. Ickes and R.F. Kidd (eds), *New Directions in Attributional Research*, Volume 3, pp. 279–305. Hillsdale, New Jersey: Lawrence Erlbaum.

Taylor, William. 1990. "The Business of Innovation: An Interview with Paul Cook," *Harvard Business Review (HBR)*, 68(March–April, 2): 97–106.

———. 1991. "The Logic of Global Business: An Interview with ABB's Percy Barnevik", *Harvard Business Review (HBR)*, 69(March–April, 2): 91–105.

The Economist. 1991. "Jack Welch Reinvents General Electric—Again", *The Economist*, London, March 30: 59–60.

———. 2001. "Link in the Global Chain", *The Economists*, London, June 2: 62–63.

———. 2004. "Business: Cigarettes and Virtual Cathedrals; Face Value", *The Economist*, London, June 5: 59.

Tichy, N.M. and S. Sherman. 1992. *Control Your Destiny or Someone Else Will: How Jack Welch is Making General Electric the World's Most Competitive Corporation.* New York: Currency/Doubleday.

Tichy, Neol and Ram Charan. 1989. "Speed, Simplicity, and Self-Confidence: Interview with Jack Welch", *Harvard Business Review (HBR)*, 67(September–October, 5): 112–20.

———. 1990. "Citicorp Faces the World: An Interview with John Reed", *Harvard Business Review (HBR)*, 68(November–December, 6): 137–56.

———. 1995. "The CEO as Coach: An Interview with Allied Signal's Lawrence Bossidy," *Harvard Business Review (HBR)*, 73(March–April, 2): 69–78.

Waldman, D.A. and F.J. Yammarino. 1999. "CEO Charismatic Leadership: Levels-of-Management and Levels-of-Analysis Effects", *Academy of Management Review*, 24(2): 266–85.

Walker, Rob. 2001. "Overvalued", *New Republic*. 224(25): 22–26.

Webber, A. 1991. "Crime and Management: An Interview with New York City Police Commissioner Lee P. Brown", *Harvard Business Review (HBR)*, 69(May–June, 3): 111–26.

Weiner, B., I. Frieze, A. Kukla, L. Reed, S. Rest, and R. Rosenbaum. 1972. "Perceiving the Causes of Success and Failure", in E.E. Jones, D.E. Kanouse, H.H. Kelley, R.E. Nisbett, S. Valins, and B. Weiner (eds), *Attribution: Perceiving the Causes of Behavior*, pp. 95–120. Morristown, New Jersey: General Learning Press.

Wells, S.M. 2003. *The Effect of Information Quantity and Quality on the Accuracy of Personality Judgments*, Dissertation Abstracts International: Section B: The Sciences and Engineering, 64, 1-B, 2003, 453. US: UMI.

Wetlaufer, Suzy. 1999. "Driving Change: An Interview with Ford Motor Company's Jacques Nasser," *Harvard Business Review (HBR)*, 77(March–April, 2): 76–88.

Wilhelm, C.C., A.M. Herd, and D.D. Steiner. 1993. "Attributional Conflict Between Managers and Subordinates: An Investigation of Leader Member Exchange Effects", *Journal of Organizational Behavior*, 14(6): 531–44.

Wofford, J.C. and T.N. Srinivasan 1983. "Experimental Tests of the Leader-Environment-Follower Interaction Theory of Leadership", *Organizational Behavior and Human Performance*, 32: 35–54.

Wood, R.E. and T.R. Mitchell 1981. "Manager Behavior in a Social Context: The Impact of Impression Management on Attributions and Disciplinary Actions", *Organizational Behavior and Human Performance*, 28: 356–78.

Zack, M.H. 1999. "Managing Codified Knowledge", *Sloan Management Review*, 40(Summer, 4): 45–58.

ABOUT THE AUTHOR

C. Lakshman is an independent consultant based in Pune, India. He received his PhD in Organization Studies from Southern Illinois University at Carbondale. He held prior appointments at Longwood University, Virginia State University, and Jackson State University. He was the Chair of the Organizational Behaviour and HRM Area at Indian Institute of Management, Indore. He has 16 years of rich experience in India and the United States, spanning both industry and academia. He combines his rich industrial marketing experience (Elcompo Electronics Pvt Ltd, Chennai) with teaching, training, and consulting experiences with various organizations including Arizona State University, Amrita Institute of Management, and Southern Illinois University. His list of consulting clients includes NLC Ltd, ABN Amro, Mahindra Finance, Impetus, and NTPC, among others. He specializes in Leadership and Knowledge Management issues in organizations. His most recent papers on Leadership and Knowledge Management were published in the *Journal of Management Studies* and in *Leadership and Organizational Development Journal*.